# BRANDYWINE
# AMERICAN HISTORY
# WORKBOOK

## Volume II

Brandywine Press • Maplecrest, New York

# Contents

Instructions for Students . . . . . . . . . . . . . . . . . . . . . . . . . v

14. The Civil War . . . . . . . . . . . . . . . . . . . . . . . . . . . . 1

15. Reconstructing the South . . . . . . . . . . . . . . . . . . . 15

16. Raiding the Continent . . . . . . . . . . . . . . . . . . . . . 27

17. The Search for New Frontiers . . . . . . . . . . . . . . . . 39

18. Taming the Forces of Social Change . . . . . . . . . . . 51

19. Progressive Empire and Progressive Reform . . . . . . . . . . 65

20. Of War, Money, Preachers, and Jazz . . . . . . . . . . . . . . . 75

21. Hitting Bottom and Climbing Back Up . . . . . . . . . . . . 87

22. World War II and Its Prelude . . . . . . . . . . . . . . . . 101

23. Warm Hearths and a Cold War . . . . . . . . . . . . . . . . 113

24. Politics Takes to the Streets . . . . . . . . . . . . . . . . 127

25. Vietnam—The Longest War . . . . . . . . . . . . . . . . . . 139

26. Testing the Reach of Power . . . . . . . . . . . . . . . . . 151

27. New Alignments and a New War . . . . . . . . . . . . . . 163

John McClymer: How to Study History . . . . . . . . . . . . . . 173

# INSTRUCTIONS
## for Students

The exercises in this workbook are an informal way to help you do well on quizzes and hour exams that are based on your American history survey text. Your teacher may ask you to tear off some pages along the perforations and hand them in or to turn in the entire workbook at the end of the semester. Answers to some questions may be found on the website: **www.brandywine sources.com** But it will not help you if you simply copy them into the workbook. What they can do is show you what you don't know, so you must try your hand first at the questions without benefit of the answers. Once you check your answers and fill out the parts of the workbook not on the website, you will be ready to take exams in your course. Your instructor may even include on the class tests a few of the multiple choice or other questions from this workbook.

The exercises are no substitute for a careful reading of the text by a student who thinks back at what is in print. The purpose is to sharpen that reading. The workbook concentrates on factual detail, but that is to encourage you to respect detail as a beginning toward your understanding of the larger forces of American history. If the workbook helps you to go beyond the detail, to a critical understanding of the nation's history, it will have done its task.

The longer instructions before each part of the fourteenth chapter will not be repeated in further chapters. Here are some suggestions for the use of the major exercises:

For each workbook chapter, the sections TERMS and VOCABULARY contain words and phrases that have a significant connection to the textbook chapter. Some of these are important for what they called up in the minds of Americans at some point in the nation's past. An instance is "natural rights." To an educated American of the late eighteenth century or the early nineteenth, the term would have been of enormous philosophical and moral value. Other phrases refer to more tangible things: institutions, events, laws, or whatever. Among these will be phrases that in themselves refer to no particular era, no special part of the world. "Navigable river," for example, could relate to any river of its kind in any country in any century. You will learn, however, that in the early nineteenth century rivers that could be navigated were essential to binding together the sprawling stretches of the young United States.

The section entitled PHOTOGRAPHS rests on the assumption that a view of someone or something, either caught directly in a photo or drawn or painted and then reproduced photographically, invites imaginative responses on the part of a viewer. What of the photograph of an African, imprisoned in a net, and awaiting sale as a slave? What thoughts might have possessed the victim? You will have no direct knowledge. Yet some attempt at wondering should sharpen your awareness that history has been lived, suffered, and occasionally triumphed over by such unnamed people as the photograph catches.

For the exercises labeled INDIVIDUALS, and for the TRUE FALSE and the MULTIPLE CHOICE sections, the basic requirements are self-evident. The TRUE FALSE questions that give specific numbers of people or things are intended not to encourage memorization but to make more specific and concrete your sense of a particular time in American history and to test your judgment. Note that for the MULTIPLE CHOICE questions you are asked to circle the letter before each statement that is correct and that often there is more than one correct answer.

The final section of each workbook chapter, offering topics for essays or oral reports, is the most ambitious. In few if any instances can you write a satisfactory essay on the basis of information drawn solely from the text. It is supposed that you will know before beginning a topic, or learn in the course of responding to it, how to use a library or one of the internet Web search engines. Some of the documents on **www.brandywinesources.com** should be useful. For an entire semester a student, at the direction of the instructor, may have time for only one topic drawn from one workbook chapter, or the project may be reserved for students aiming at extra credit. Or your instructor may use topics for oral discussions or brief essays in which you simply suggest how to go about a more extended response. The compilers of the workbook tried not to patronize you by assuming you are capable of nothing other than memorization or by failing to provide challenging questions in which you can exhibit to your instructor, your classmates, and yourself that you are up to the game.

This volume of American History Workbook contains, at the end, a guide to studying history and writing term papers that some instructors and students may find useful.

# The Civil War   14

**A. TERMS**—For each of these, indicate the meaning of the word or phrase.
(Your instructor may request that you tear out along the perforations some or all of the pages in this workbook and hand them in.)

federal installations _____

_____

_____

conscription _____

_____

_____

commander-in-chief _____

_____

_____

diplomatic recognition _____

_____

_____

tactical dexterity _____

_____

_____

**B. PHOTOGRAPHS**

1. Explain each of the images in the cartoon on the next page. Identify each candidate, the candidate's dancing partner, the important points of his platform, and how the person represented by the featured musician relates to the proceedings in general.

_____

_____

_____

_____

_____

_____

_____

_____

_____

2.  The twentieth-century black militant Malcolm X, asked at some time prior to his pilgrimage to Mecca whether there was any white man he respected, would reply "John Brown." Frederick Douglass remarked that Brown's commitment to abolition was greater than Douglass's own. Citizens of Harpers Ferry drove Brown's little force into an engine house until marines could capture him. Virginia hanged John Brown as a traitor. Write either an indictment of John Brown or a eulogy for him, written from the perspective of someone living at the time he lived, using studies and sources of facts available to you today. A particularly helpful book on Brown has been edited by John Stauffer (Brandywine Press, 2003).

**C. VOCABULARY**—For each of these, indicate the meaning of the word as used in the chapter.

homestead _____

_____

_____

arsenal _____

_____

_____

daguerreotype _____

_____

_____

ironclad _____

_____

_____

contraband _____

_____

_____

greenbacks _____

_____

_____

sanitation _____

_____

_____

chloroform _____

_____

_____

copperheads _____

_____

_____

**D. INDIVIDUALS**—Identify each of these people.

John Brown _____

_____

_____

Mary Chesnut _____

_____

_____

Joseph Hooker _____

_____

_____

Robert E. Lee _____

_____

_____

Jefferson Davis _____

_____

George B. McClellan _____

_____

William S. Rosecrans _____

_____

Irvin McDowell _____

_____

Jubal Early _____

_____

Philip Sheridan _____

_____

William Tecumseh Sherman _____

_____

Nathan Bedford Forrest _____

_____

Ambrose E. Burnside _____

_____

John C. Breckinridge _____

_____

John Bell Hood _____

_____

P. T. G. Beauregard _____

_____

John Bell _____

_____

Joseph E. Johnston _____

_____

_____

George G. Meade _____

_____

_____

James Longstreet _____

_____

_____

Benjamin Butler _____

_____

_____

Clement L. Vallandigham _____

_____

_____

Thomas J. Jackson _____

_____

_____

Ulysses S. Grant _____

_____

_____

J. E. B. Stuart _____

_____

_____

Elizabeth Blackwell _____

_____

_____

## E. TRUE FALSE—circle one.

1. T   F   The Republican Party platform of 1860 appealed to northern race prejudice, through measures that would settle white homesteaders in the West, excluding large plantations, slaves, and, at least by implication, free African Americans.
2. T   F   After the 1860 presidential election, a convention in South Carolina requested that Lincoln clarify his position toward slavery in the states where it was then legal, and suggested it might vote to secede from the Union if his response was not satisfactory.
3. T   F   The Confederate Constitution of 1861 was in large part modeled on the United States Constitution of 1787, but explicitly protected "the institution of Negro slavery."
4. T   F   Abraham Lincoln made a triumphal entry into Washington, D.C., for his inauguration.
5. T   F   Major Robert Anderson, commanding officer at Fort Sumter, opened an artillery barrage on South Carolina militia in Charleston harbor, provoking a Confederate counterattack.
6. T   F   President Lincoln issued a call in April 1861 for seventy-five thousand militia volunteers to serve for ninety days in suppressing insurrection against the United States.
7. T   F   Military conflict between Union and Confederate forces began on July 21, 1861, at the Battle of Bull Run in eastern Virginia.

8.  T  F  Secretary of State Seward announced that because secession was illegal, Confederate soldiers captured by the Union army would be prosecuted for treason and insurrection.

9.  T  F  General George B. McClellan did an expert job of training, drilling, and organizing the Army of the Potomac, but Lincoln was disappointed at McClellan's hesitation to take the army into combat.

10.  T  F  An important victory for the federal blockade of the Confederate coastline was the capture of Roanoke Island in North Carolina by a Union army under command of General Ambrose E. Burnside.

11.  T  F  The *Trent* affair began when two Confederate agents under British diplomatic passports were captured outside a historic mansion in the New Jersey state capital.

12.  T  F  For the manufacture of gunpowder, United States military forces during the Civil War depended on imports of saltpeter from India, which was ruled by Britain.

13.  T  F  One argument for freeing slaves, as a wartime policy, was to deprive the Confederacy of badly needed labor to replace that of white men called up for military service.

14.  T  F  The Homestead Act of 1860 offered a 160-acre plot of federal land to any man or woman who lived on it for five years and improved it by cultivation or building.

15.  T  F  Land grant colleges got their name because they were built in various states on land granted by the federal government for the purpose of establishing schools.

16.  T  F  The Emancipation Proclamation abolished slavery throughout the United States.

17.  T  F  Democrats who favored immediate peace with the Confederacy denounced a war of emancipation as an assault on the freedoms of white Americans.

18.  T  F  Rank and file Confederate soldiers denounced draft exemptions for large slaveowners as a sign that the Confederacy was run for the benefit of the rich.

19.  T  F  In the northern states the Democratic Party ran a racist campaign in 1864, attacking emancipation, denouncing Lincoln as wasting white lives in the cause of black freedom.

20.  T  F  Lee retired from the Battle of Gettysburg with almost as many troops in the Army of Northern Virginia as when the battle began.

21.  T  F  In the defense of the federal garrison at Milliken's Bend on the Mississippi River above Vicksburg, soldiers of African descent demonstrated their fighting ability.

22.  T  F  In the fall of 1863 northern public opinion, inspired by the New York draft riots and the fighting around Vicksburg, turned sharply against abolition of slavery.

23.  T  F  Copperhead victories in the elections for governor in Ohio and Pennsylvania undermined support for Lincoln's government in 1863.

24.  T  F  A Unionist majority in eastern Tennessee lived under Confederate military occupation until the summer of 1863.

25.  T  F  In May 1864 Confederate cavalry under General Jubal Early reached the northern suburbs of Washington, D.C.

26.  T  F  In 1864 Maryland and Missouri voted for the Democratic presidential candidate George McClellan, while Delaware, New Jersey, and Kentucky voted to reelect Lincoln.

27.  T  F  The demands of the Civil War strained northern industry beyond endurance, while wartime need spurred a great growth in southern manufacturing.

28.  T  F  One measure no Confederate official or general would ever consider during the entire war was enlisting African Americans as soldiers in the rebel army.

**F. MATCHING** Match the name of each battle listed below with its significance to the course of the war.

SELF-TEST QUESTIONS
(matching, true/false, multiple choice)
**The answers will be found on the Brandywine website:**
www.brandywinesources.com

___ Fredericksburg

f)  Emancipation Proclamation issued after Lee's invasion turned back

___ Vicksburg

d)  defeat of Lee's last invasion of the North after three-day battle

____Antietam

____Atlanta

____Chancellorsville

____First Bull Run

____Petersburg

____Wilderness

____Gettysburg

____Missionary Ridge

____Mobile Bay

____Shiloh

____Peninsular Campaign

____Chickamauga Creek

a) slaughter of thousands of Union soldiers in an assault that accomplished nothing

m) clear-cut victory for Confederate forces showed that the war would be long

j) stopped Confederate attempt to chase federal army out of Tennessee

h) McClellan moved slowly, fought cautiously, outmaneuvered by Lee

l) sealed off one of the last remaining Confederate ports in 1864

c) Lee out-thinks, out-fights, and out-flanks Joseph Hooker

e) broke the last Confederate position on the Mississippi River

g) the fighting there aided in securing Union control of Chattanooga

k) Confederate attempt to reenter eastern Tennessee was barely repulsed

n) heavy Union losses, but the army pressed forward instead of retreating

b) cost the Confederacy its main transportation hub and a lot of its industry

i) last major battle, ending with Lee's flight, followed by surrender

## G. MULTIPLE CHOICE—circle one or more correct answers.

1. In the division of the popular and electoral votes among the four major candidates for president of the United States in 1860,
   a) Lincoln won a majority of the popular vote and three quarters of the Electoral College.
   b) Stephen Douglas won the second largest number of popular votes, but took the smallest number of votes in the Electoral College.
   c) Lincoln won the largest number of popular votes and a huge majority in the Electoral College.
   d) John C. Breckinridge won eighteen percent of the popular vote, and John Bell even less, but each won more votes in the Electoral College than Douglas.
   e) Lincoln finished in last place in the popular vote, but won a majority of votes in the Electoral College.

2. Between the election of November 1860 and Lincoln's inauguration in March 1861,
   a) seven states from South Carolina to Texas declared that they were no longer part of the Union.
   b) Virginia, Tennessee, North Carolina, and Arkansas joined the Confederacy.
   c) President James Buchanan denied that states had a legal right to secede, but said that he could find no way to stop them.
   d) Confederate troops in Charleston, South Carolina, fired on Fort Sumter.
   e) the Republican leader William Seward described President Buchanan as having announced that he had a duty to enforce the law unless anyone objected.

3. Upon his becoming president, Lincoln's initial response to secession included
   a) immediate enlistment of one million soldiers to invade the seceded states.
   b) a promise not to interfere with slavery in states where it existed, though he rejected a proposal to allow slavery in territories south of the Missouri Compromise line.
   c) endorsement of a secret proposal to go to war with France and Spain, as a tactic to reunite the country.
   d) securing federal installations located in seceded states, so that in event of armed conflict the Confederacy would be the aggressor.
   e) resupplying the federal garrison at Fort Sumter, South Carolina, and notifying state authorities of his intention to do so.

4. Among the northernmost states that allowed slavery as of 1861,
   a) Missouri's governor remained loyal to the Union, but rebels took over most of the state and held Missouri throughout the war.
   b) militias for and against secession were organized in Kentucky, but most residents of the state remained loyal to the Union.
   c) western North Carolina and eastern Tennessee were mostly loyal to the Union, rebelling against state governments and sending volunteers to the federal army.

    d) Massachusetts volunteers heading for Washington to defend the capital against Confederate forces were enthusiastically greeted as they passed through Maryland.

    e) support for secession from the state of Virginia was strong in the mountainous western region: federal troops and local Unionists drove out Confederate forces.

5. The first Battle of Bull Run, also known as Manassas,
    a) resulted in a stunning Union victory that led to hopes for an early end to the war.
    b) was fought on both sides by soldiers who lacked training and experience.
    c) gave General Thomas Jackson the nickname "Stonewall" for keeping his brigade of Virginia soldiers steady in breaking a federal assault.
    d) made Robert E. Lee famous as commanding general of Confederate forces.
    e) ended in a defeat of federal forces, at the end of a hard day's fighting by both sides.

6. Material advantages held by states loyal to the Union against the Confederacy included
    a) a population of nine million in the seceded states, of whom a third consisted of slaves.
    b) a tradition of military service and training, which produced a hardened combat force more powerful than the southern sense of honor could deliver.
    c) a diverse economy with abundant industry, also self-sufficient in food.
    d) the sympathy of the British government, which because it had patrolled the Atlantic for fifty years to suppress the slave trade would never think of aiding the Confederacy.
    e) a navy to deploy in a blockade of Confederate ports, while the Confederacy depended on foreign trade to sustain its economy.

7. Years of fighting in northern Virginia between Washington and Richmond changed little, while in the western theater of the Civil War, by the end of 1862
    a) Confederate cavalry raided deep into northern Ohio and Illinois, greeted by people holding strong southern sympathies.
    b) Union forces moved up the Tennessee and Cumberland rivers from Illinois, taking forts Henry and Donelson and the city of Nashville, and winning the Battle of Shiloh.
    c) Texas, Louisiana, and Arkansas voted to rejoin the United States, prevented only by Confederate military occupation under General Albert Sidney Johnston.
    d) New Orleans fell to a Union naval force that cut off Confederate river traffic on the Mississippi from the Gulf of Mexico.
    e) a Confederate invasion of Kentucky under General Braxton Bragg was turned back at Perryville in October.

8. Confederate hopes for diplomatic recognition from Britain and France depended on
    a) powerful Confederate military victories, showing that the South could win.
    b) dependence of British textile industries on imported cotton, which could motivate Britain to break the blockade of southern ports.
    c) French intervention in Mexico, which would gain from a permanent split in the United States and Confederate support of the French presence in Mexico.
    d) whether slavery became an issue of the war; Britain could not openly support the Confederacy if the Union government made emancipation a war policy.
    e) large bribes demanded by French government officials from Confederate diplomats, privately referred to as the "little x, y, z affair."

9. The evolution of United States military policy toward slavery included these steps:
    a) On April 3, 1861, Lincoln issued an executive order that any slaves encountered by federal military forces would be "henceforth and forever free."
    b) General Benjamin Butler took in fugitive slaves, arguing that as property of rebels, they were "contraband of war"; and since Union officers refused to hold them as property, they should be considered free.

c) In 1862 Congress prohibited the return of fugitive slaves to their owners, then offered financial support to any state adopting a gradual end to slavery.

d) Fugitive slaves reaching federal lines were organized into caravans and sent to Lawrence, Kansas, for resettlement on reservations.

e) A militia act in late 1862 authorized the president to enlist men of African ancestry into the military.

10. Draft riots in New York City in 1863 were motivated in part by
    a) hostility among Irish immigrant laborers toward New York residents of African descent, many of whom sought the same low-paid jobs as the Irish.
    b) anger at conscription for military service and the belief that only the poorer classes were actually called up.
    c) resentment toward employers who were hostile to labor unions.
    d) a determination to have the government of the United States submit to the Pope.
    e) wrath directed at Protestant churches.

11. Popular resentment by civilians of Confederate government policy took the form of
    a) massive nonviolent antiwar protests in Atlanta, New Orleans, and Richmond.
    b) resistance to decrees that farmers must turn over a portion of crops, meat, and dairy products to the government.
    c) bread riots in major southern cities, where women invaded shops selling food and took whatever they needed.
    d) repeated assassination attempts targeting members of Jefferson Davis's cabinet.
    e) a virtual secession from Confederate law by areas opposed to conscription.

12. In his campaigns in command of the Army of the Potomac, Grant
    a) was so arrogant that he ignored direction from President Lincoln and at times refused even to speak to his commander-in-chief.
    b) continued his offensive against the Army of Northern Virginia after each battle, regardless of his losses in the previous fighting.
    c) paused for long periods of time between battles to reprovision his soldiers and think over what he wanted to do next.
    d) forced the Confederate forces from one defensive position to another.
    e) was racing to win victories faster than Sherman, his lifelong rival and enemy.

13. When General William Tecumseh Sherman captured Atlanta from Confederate troops,
    a) he was victorious in a long campaign of maneuvering around entrenched Confederate positions that could not be taken by frontal assault.
    b) his soldiers indiscriminately slaughtered the civilian population of the city.
    c) the victory improved Lincoln's chances of reelection by northern voters.
    d) the Confederate general Hood tried to move north and cut Sherman's supply lines to Tennessee, but Sherman decided to forget the supply lines and live off the land.
    e) the entire city was dismantled and put into storage, not to be seen again until it was pulled out for use as a backdrop in making movies eighty years later.

14. On the disposal of black prisoners of war,
    a) neither the federal command nor the Confederate officers had any interest in treating African Americans as soldiers once they were captured.
    b) federal troops taken prisoner by Confederate armies refused to live in the same prisoner-of-war camps with African American prisoners.
    c) in 1863, Confederate armies refused to treat African Americans as prisoners of war, or exchange them on equal terms for white soldiers.
    d) the federal government refused to exchange any prisoners unless all federal soldiers were treated the same, and this decision increased the numbers kept in prisoner compounds.
    e) not until January 1865 did the Confederate government agree that all African Americans captured in battle, in federal uniform, were prisoners of war.

15. Sanitation and medical knowledge had what impact on the lives of Civil War soldiers?
    a) The first cholera epidemic to reach the United States forced General McClellan to keep the Army of the Potomac in camp for most of 1862.
    b) At the time the medical profession was ignorant of the microorganisms causing infection, and despite some serious attempts at teaching cleanliness to the troops, disease killed more soldiers than battlefield combat.
    c) Advanced scientific and technical ability kept federal soldiers quite healthy, while Confederate soldiers, paying no attention to cleanliness, died of infectious disease.
    d) The United States Sanitary Commission was organized to recruit nurses, obtain medical supplies, and teach better hygienic methods to soldiers.
    e) To stop the spread of gangrene from infected wounds, physicians of that time had no measure available except amputation.

## H. ESSAY QUESTIONS OR ORAL REPORTS
    FOR MANY QUESTIONS IN THIS WORKBOOK THE PRIMARY SOURCES ON THE INTERNET SITE **www.brandywinesources.com** WILL BE HELPFUL.

    You will not find the answers to all of these questions in your textbook. Particularly for oral reports, you will have to look up more specialized sources. For most essay questions, moreover, there is no "correct" answer. This is an opportunity to present your own opinion, with one important consideration: Cite a documented source for anything you quote or assert unless the fact or interpretation is generally known. You should give your own opinion such weight as information and analysis support. These instructions will not be repeated for similar questions pertaining to other chapters in this workbook.

1. On the question of allowing slavery in federal territories, in the District of Columbia, and in states where slavery was prohibited, consider the applicability of constitutional guarantees, more specifically the Fifth Amendment, protecting private property from seizure or interference by the federal government. Was the Supreme Court under Chief Justice Roger Taney legally correct when it ruled that slaves were property, and that property in slaves was an individual right of the slaveowner?

2. Present an argument as to what Abraham Lincoln's own inner political motivations were during his presidency. Examine his presidential actions, the circumstances surrounding each, and the results they led to in the long term. Did he intend to abolish slavery, and use the war to bring reluctant northern public opinion around to the idea? Or was he genuinely motivated only by a desire to save the Union, speaking to questions of slavery and race only when it served the interest of federal supremacy?

3. Can a government "conceived in liberty, and dedicated to the proposition that all men are created equal" be strong enough to defend itself against insurrection and foreign enemies? What freedoms and constitutional guarantees did the Union government set aside in order to save the republic?

4. Examine the Civil War career of General George B. McClellan. Provide your own analysis of how he might better have handled his responsibility for the Army of the Potomac. Or make a case that he was following the right course. In the course of your investigation, refer to McClellan's own writings, and the writings of Lincoln and others in the government.

5. Prepare an economic overview of the world market for cotton from 1859 through 1867. In what regions worldwide was cultivation well established and where was it just beginning? Decide what the possibilities were of the Confederacy's pressuring Britain into diplomatic recognition and a naval assault against the Union blockade for the sake of keeping the flow of southern cotton to British factories.

6. Pick a battle of the Civil War and write a detailed analysis of why it began as it did, the options that each commanding officer had at critical points as the battle developed, and why each made the choices he did.

_____
_____
_____
_____
_____
_____
_____
_____
_____
_____
_____
_____
_____
_____
_____
_____
_____
_____
_____
_____
_____
_____
_____
_____
_____
_____
_____
_____
_____
_____
_____
_____
_____
_____

# Reconstructing the South 15

## A. TERMS

Freedmen's Bureau _____
_____
_____

forty acres and a mule _____
_____
_____

Reconstruction _____
_____
_____

market capitalism _____
_____
_____

gang labor _____
_____
_____

harmony of capital and labor _____
_____
_____

Black Codes _____
_____
_____

republican government _____
_____
_____

civil rights _____
_____
_____

due process of law _____
_____
_____

white supremacy _____

_____

_____

equal protection of the laws _____

_____

_____

states' rights _____

_____

_____

## B. PHOTOGRAPHS

1. Look up George Washington's and Abraham Lincoln's own writings on the subject of slavery, mostly to be found in personal correspondence. Have them discuss the subject.

2. Write a summary of the formation of the Ku Klux Klan and its activity during Reconstruction. In its origins the KKK murdered Republicans, voted for Democrats, and prided itself on its resistance to the policies of the victorious United States. The revived Klan of the 1920s celebrated loyalty to the United States. It allied itself with Republicans and Democrats who supported the Eighteenth Amendment prohibiting the manufacture and sale of alcohol. And it directed much of its hatred against Roman Catholics, Jews, and immigrants from central and eastern Europe. It was white supremacist, but African Americans were not its single obsession. Write a brief essay comparing the two Klans, examining why the second Klan took on the character it did and why Catholics, Jews, the newer waves of immigrants, and violators of Prohibition were its chosen targets. Suggest why the second Klan, different in so many ways from the Klan of Reconstruction days, nonetheless thought itself to be the descendant of that first KKK.

_____
_____
_____
_____
_____
_____
_____
_____

3. Note the political climate of 1872 and the career of Thomas Nast. Then write a summary of what the cartoon on the next page represented at the time. What politics was Horace Greeley endorsing by 1872, and what was the position his political faction took toward Reconstruction? Note also that the figure standing beside the Klansman is Irish. The facial features became stereotypical for portrayals of the Irish and would survive into the popular and friendlier Maggie and Jiggs newspaper comic strip of the twentieth century. Why does Nast make the Irish into allies of the Klan? Think of events in New York City in the summer of 1863, and remember that the Irish voted Democratic.

## C. VOCABULARY

Johnson's "Swing Around the Circle" _____

_____

_____

freedmen _____

_____

sharecropping _____

_____

peonage _____

_____

impeachment _____

_____

carpetbaggers _____

_____

scalawags _____

_____

ten-percent plan _____

_____

pocket veto _____

_____

terrorism _____

_____

crop lien _____

_____

## D. INDIVIDUALS

Oliver Otis Howard _____

_____

Andrew Johnson _____

_____

John Wilkes Booth _____
_____
_____

Alexander Stephens _____
_____
_____

Thaddeus Stevens _____
_____
_____

Horatio Seymour _____
_____
_____

Lucy Stone _____
_____
_____

Thomas Nast _____
_____
_____

Susan B. Anthony _____
_____
_____

Elizabeth Cady Stanton _____
_____
_____

Horace Greeley _____
_____
_____

Benjamin Butler _____
_____
_____

## E. TRUE FALSE—circle one.

1. T  F  All slaves throughout the country were officially free as of April 9, 1865, following Robert E. Lee's surrender at Appomattox.
2. T  F  Tennessee, according to the status the Union defined for the state, abolished slavery by law in 1863.
3. T  F  Most black southerners in 1870 lived in a two-parent home.
4. T  F  As a result of the Emancipation Proclamation, slaves became free when the Union army conquered rebel territory in which they were held as slaves.
5. T  F  Sharecropping was a status for freed blacks, not for white farmers.
6. T  F  Early after the end of the Civil War southern militia units, some wearing Confederate uniforms, patrolled the countryside in former Confederate states enforcing Black Codes.
7. T  F  Emancipation was bewildering for both freed slaves and their former owners.

8. T F Federal officials encouraged freed slaves to leave the plantations and take to the road.
9. T F President Andrew Johnson identified with the southern plantation owning class.
10. T F Some former slaves, knowing how helpless their former owners were at the prospect of survival by working, attempted to help them out.
11. T F The Congress elected in 1866 denied seats to southern representatives and senators elected by new southern state governments endorsed by President Johnson.
12. T F John Tyler, a former president of the United States, held a public office within the Confederacy, and if he had survived the war the Fourteenth Amendment would have barred him from federal office unless Congress removed the restriction.
13. T F Andrew Johnson's hostility to the slave-owning planter class made him friendly toward the rights of the freed slaves.
14. T F Tennessee refused to ratify the Fourteenth Amendment.
15. T F A North Carolina planter was upset when a black veteran of the Union bowed and greeted him.
16. T F Land was taken from plantation owners as a matter of federal policy, and distributed to freed slaves so they could support themselves.
17. T F James Longstreet, a former Confederate general, led opposition to Reconstruction policies, and fomented white riots in New Orleans.
18. T F Much of the political leadership among African Americans after the Civil War came from blacks who had been free since birth and were accustomed to some independence.
19. T F During Reconstruction, blacks were a minority of the voters in South Carolina.
20. T F In the 1868 elections, the Ku Klux Klan assassinated elected officials and terrorized black and white Republican voters, with the object of defeating Horatio Seymour in the presidential election.

## F. MULTIPLE CHOICE—circle one or more correct answers.

1. Among the many responses of freed slaves to emancipation was
   a) an effort to establish a gang system that would continue their familiar work patterns but without rule by slaveowners.
   b) a mixture of exaltation and sadness, affection for former owners, and a desire to lash out at them.
   c) setting out on the road to find children, parents, or spouses who had been separated from them by sale years before.
   d) forming guerrilla bands who systematically looted and burned plantations.
   e) flocking to port cities seeking ships to take them back to Africa.

2. Among the responses of slaveowners to the emancipation of their human property were these:
   a) shock that slaves thought to be happy and faithful would leave, once free to do so.
   b) a determination to divide up plantations among the slaves who had worked on them.
   c) a frenzy of whippings and other violence against their slaves, taking out their bitterness and frustration at loss of the war and anger at imminent emancipation.
   d) a general desire to drive all the freed slaves into the northern states.
   e) an invitation to their former slaves to formal meetings at which the two races could get better acquainted on an equal basis.

3. Union soldiers who brought the Emancipation Proclamation to a plantation might be
   a) committed abolitionists.
   b) white racists with no interest in freeing slaves.
   c) African Americans enlisted after 1862.
   d) Santee Lakota, afraid a Confederate victory would cost them their land.
   e) whites who became abolitionists when they saw the scars on the backs of slaves.

4. The market ideology of the Republican Party, which shaped programs for freed slaves,
   a) sought to build a nation of independent, self-sufficient small farmers.
   b) insisted that private property in land should not be disturbed or redistributed.
   c) advocated a diversified southern economy, breaking dependence on cotton.

    d) believed that a labor force working for wages was better than a population of families owning a piece of land and using it for subsistence.

    e) expected human beings to be hungry for possessions as a main incentive in life.

5. These were among responses on the part of northern economic interests to the postwar situation in the South:

    a) Factory owners donated millions of dollars to educational and welfare programs.

    b) Missionaries from New England taught economic self-sufficiency to freed slaves.

    c) Clothing mill owners needed endless amounts of southern cotton, so they did not want to see the land used to grow food for southern families.

    d) The northern economy was hiring massive numbers of factory hands overseen by floor superintendents, shaping a workforce similar to gang labor in the southern fields.

    e) Businesses seeking to invest in southern states expected that hiring freedmen would provide them with a more loyal workforce than hiring Confederate veterans.

6. President Lincoln's plan for Reconstruction provided that

    a) Confederate states be kept under martial law for a minimum of ten years, subject to curfews and suspension of the writ of habeas corpus.

    b) at least ten percent of white male residents in a state that had been militarily subdued must take an oath of future loyalty to the Union.

    c) slavery must be gradually ended over a period of thirty years and all children be freed at the age of eighteen.

    d) before a state could resume its own government and send representatives to Congress, it must adopt a constitution abolishing slavery.

    e) any state that had attempted to secede must pay the federal government in specie for the expense that state had cost the federal government by warring on the nation.

7. The Wade-Davis plan passed by Congress and pocket-vetoed by Lincoln required that

    a) half of a seceded state's white male population pledge loyalty to the Union.

    b) each seceded state provide financing through bond sales for a massive program of railroad building across the South.

    c) citizens who could take the Ironclad Oath that they had never supported secession elect delegates to a convention to draw up a state constitution.

    d) at least half the congressional districts in each seceded state have a black majority.

    e) each seceded state grant blacks equality before the law; but the plan had no requirement that equality include the right to vote.

8. During the year of President Andrew Johnson's Reconstruction plan,

    a) estates of any planter owning more than twenty slaves were confiscated and sold.

    b) most rebels received blanket pardons if they pledged loyalty to the Union and support for emancipation.

    c) the Ku Klux Klan was recognized as the president's primary agency for establishing Reconstruction government in former Confederate states.

    d) Johnson attempted to keep enough readmitted states from ratifying the Thirteenth Amendment that it would be defeated.

    e) officials of the defeated Confederate government were elected to Congress, including Alexander Stephens of Georgia, vice president of the Confederacy.

9. Among Black Codes adopted by states President Johnson readmitted to the Union in 1865, typical rules

    a) granted blacks legal rights to marry, hold property, and have some access to the courts.

    b) provided payments to former slaves equivalent to back wages for their last ten years of slave labor.

    c) required black residents to show proof each January of employment for the year.

d) prohibited workers from leaving a plantation without permission from their employer.

e) were consistent in defining blacks alone as the object of their controls.

10. The Reconstruction Plan adopted by Congress in 1867 over President Johnson's veto
    a) disenfranchised all voters in seceded states except for blacks and carpetbaggers.
    b) divided the region from Virginia to Texas into five military districts.
    c) imposed no direct federal rule in Tennessee, already readmitted to the Union.
    d) allocated money for crop price support payments to depressed plantation owners.
    e) required, as conditions for readmitting a former secessionist state, that the state ratify the Fourteenth Amendment and adopt a state constitution giving adult male blacks the vote.

11. Among people in former Confederate states who might support Republican policies were
    a) wealthy industrialists who had opposed the secession effected by their enemies, the cotton planters.
    b) Choctaw, Cherokee, and Seminole.
    c) freed slaves, once their right to vote was firmly established by law.
    d) people in hill and mountain areas who resented domination by wealthy planters.
    e) residents of the lowlands angry at the apparent privileges the Confederacy had given to the rich, or resentful of the misery that secession and war had brought to the South.

12. Delegates to state constitutional conventions in former Confederate states
    a) represented carpetbaggers and freed slaves alone, excluding native white voters.
    b) were elected under laws excluding former Confederate officials, which led many former rebels to refuse to participate in the elections at all.
    c) came in large numbers from the ranks of southern white Unionists and mountaineers.
    d) included carpetbaggers, who made up about one sixth of the total.
    e) united white and black delegates for a program of complete racial equality.

13. Measures popular among southern state constitutional convention delegates included
    a) the first provision for free public education, but in schools separated by race.
    b) plans to prevent freed slaves from voting that were not too obvious.
    c) a general tax on property that increased the levy on landowners.
    d) restricting the power of ex-rebel planters, a policy favored by hill country white Unionists.
    e) immediately replacing all federal troops with local law enforcement.

14. During the period of Klan violence,
    a) the KKK, to give itself an air of respectability, organized charitable relief for widows and orphans of Confederate veterans.
    b) the Klan engaged in whipping, shooting, and hanging known Republican voters, to intimidate both black and white supporters of Reconstruction.
    c) a militia of white Unionists and blacks organized by Arkansas Governor Powell Clayton tried Klan suspects by military commission.
    d) the Klan toured northern states with colorfully costumed vaudeville acts to patch up wartime differences and give a positive view of southern life.
    e) a landowner who had distributed land to his former slaves was whipped, and African Americans who owned or rented their own land were under threat.

15. Political trends and influences that helped bring an end to Reconstruction included
    a) a widespread belief in Congress that the Thirteenth Amendment had been a mistake.
    b) a conviction that the Constitution as amended during Reconstruction provided southern African Americans all the protection they needed.
    c) evangelical revivals that persuaded black voters to abandon political action.
    d) loss of interest by northern voters in the rights of southern African Americans.
    e) a determination on the part of Liberal Republicans to end attacks on "the better sort of people" such as they thought they saw in proposals for inflated currency benefiting labor.

## G. ESSAY QUESTIONS OR ORAL REPORTS

1. Write what you think should have been the right plan for Reconstruction of the defeated seces-sionist states. Define the goals of the plan. Then define what groups in the various former Confederate states might have rallied in support of the plan, and what groups, if any, would have to be crushed or subdued to make it work. Finally, how would your plan have been put into action? What political, economic, and military forces would have to be mobilized?

2. Do some research into how citizens who had remained loyal to the Union within seceded states, or remained apart from the Confederate government, lived in the years after the Civil War. Consider the kinds of people who had been hostile to secession and major geographic areas that resisted Confederate rule. Detail examples of support of emancipation and opposi-tion to it, as well as attitudes toward Black Codes, Reconstruction governments, and Ku Klux Klan activity.

3. Examine how the racial attitudes that took hold after Reconstruction, and gave rise to Jim Crow laws, were cultivated during the 1870s and 1880s to win back white voters who had given support to Republican state governments in the South. This will require some examples of racist rhetoric used, who used it, and in what year, set in chronological order. Where and why did Republican administrations win the support of southern white voters? Who was most motivated to try to break that support?

4. Examine any two leading Liberal Republicans. Look at their politics going back before the Civil War, and see how their thought evolved in response to the war and Reconstruction. Can you say of any of them that they betrayed their earlier principles, or was there some consis-tency in the development of their thought?

5. Thousands of individuals who made important contributions to Reconstruction are not named in this chapter: teachers, entrepreneurs, governors, sheriffs, congressmen, soldiers, farmers, to mention a few. Look up some of them, select one or more, and prepare a biographical or his-torical summary of the life and accomplishments of whoever you have chosen. Relate the experiences that brought your choice or choices to the events of Reconstruction. What changes may the Civil War and Reconstruction have made in the views and motivations of your one or more individuals?

# Raiding the Continent

**16**

## A. TERMS

ghost dance _____
_____

grandfather clause _____
_____

vertical integration _____
_____

Gilded Age _____
_____

"white race" _____
_____

eight-hour day movement _____
_____

mining the soil _____
_____

Anglo-Saxon _____
_____

civil service _____
_____

resource extraction _____
_____

wage slavery _____

_____

_____

horizontal integration _____

_____

_____

separate but equal _____

_____

_____

woman suffrage _____

_____

_____

organized leisure _____

_____

_____

## B. PHOTOGRAPHS

1. What philosophy motivated the Knights of Labor to accept African Americans as full participants in the labor movement? What practical considerations made this acceptable within the organization, despite the end of Reconstruction? Why were other labor organizations racially exclusive?

_____

_____

_____

_____

_____

_____

_____

_____

_____

_____

_____

_____

_____

_____

_____

_____

_____

_____

_____

_____

_____

_____

_____

_____

_____

_____

_____

_____

_____

_____

_____

_____

**2.** Write a half page suggesting to the best of your imagination what would have been the thoughts of the individuals in this picture, liberated not many years ago from slavery, moving from the inhospitable South to a destination in the Midwest new to them, exercising a freedom to do so that would earlier have been unimaginable.

_____

_____

_____

_____

_____

_____

_____

_____

_____

_____

_____

_____

_____

_____

_____

_____

_____

_____

_____

_____

_____

3. Consider and write down some of the advantages of polygamy from the viewpoint of women in Mormon society, and some of the disadvantages. Try to think from the viewpoint of nineteenth-century culture, not that of the twenty-first. In a frontier setting, would the need for large families be a strong argument for polygamy? What of the argument of nineteenth-century opponents of slavery that polygamy amounted to the enslavement of women?

_____

_____

_____

_____

_____

_____

_____

_____

_____
_____
_____
_____
_____
_____
_____
_____
_____
_____
_____
_____
_____
_____
_____
_____
_____
_____
_____
_____
_____

## C. VOCABULARY

exposition _____
_____

air brake _____
_____

wilderness _____
_____

monopoly _____
_____

blacklist _____
_____

capitalism _____
_____

Exodusters _____
_____

## D. INDIVIDUALS

George Custer _____

_____

_____

Tatanka Yotanka (Sitting Bull) _____

_____

_____

Rutherford B. Hayes _____

_____

_____

Terence Powderly _____

_____

_____

Chief Joseph _____

_____

_____

Goyathlay (Geronimo) _____

_____

_____

William "Buffalo Bill" Cody _____

_____

_____

John Sherman _____

_____

_____

Jay Gould _____

_____

_____

Joseph Pulitzer _____

_____

_____

Elizabeth Cady Stanton _____

_____

_____

Susan B. Anthony _____

_____

_____

Arthur Conan Doyle _____

_____

_____

## E. ORGANIZATIONS

Knights of Labor _____
_____
_____

American Federation of Labor _____
_____
_____

Grange _____
_____
_____

Farmers' Alliances _____
_____
_____

Colored Farmers' National Alliance _____
_____
_____

National League _____
_____
_____

Populist Party _____
_____
_____

American Woman Suffrage Association _____
_____
_____

National Woman Suffrage Association _____
_____
_____

Grand Army of the Republic _____
_____
_____

## F. TRUE FALSE—circle one.

1. T  F   Racial equality and inclusion were a notable feature of the 1876 Centennial Exposition, which made much of African American contributions to science, military service, and education.
2. T  F   At Wounded Knee, South Dakota, in 1890, the Seventh Cavalry responded to the ghost dance religion by slaughtering every Lakota Indian in sight.
3. T  F   One of the first books to challenge the record of lying, cheating, and mismanagement of Indian affairs by the United States was *A Century of Dishonor* by Helen Hunt Jackson.
4. T  F   After 1877, racial lines between whites and blacks, Indians, Asians, and Latinos hardened.
5. T  F   During the 1870s and 1880s, workers were freed from the drudgery of craft labor in individual shops, and provided with the security of steady factory employment.

6. T F The Chinese Exclusion Act of 1882 allowed large numbers of Chinese immigrants to enter the United States, when immigration from most nations was strictly limited.

7. T F In 1882 Thomas Edison succeeded in lighting the Wall Street financial district.

8. T F In the late nineteenth century, courts ruled that wages were the result of an individual contract between employer and employee, and rejected efforts among workers to organize and bargain as a group.

9. T F Terence Powderly, as Grand Master of the Knights of Labor, opposed strikes as futile, short-term endeavors that distracted members from long-range goals.

10. T F The American Federation of Labor denounced collective bargaining for better wages and shorter hours as a surrender to capitalism, and instead prepared for a nationwide general strike.

11. T F Plains Indians had hunted the buffalo to near extinction until college-educated naturalists began to hop off transcontinental trains to secure the few survivors to breed.

12. T F Farmers settling the Great Plains as Indians were cleared off the land were self-sufficient in all foods each family needed, bartering a small surplus and selling very little.

13. T F Old-stock Americans differed on whether to assimilate immigrants into American life and culture.

14. T F As Jim Crow laws were adopted during the quarter century following Reconstruction, African Americans were rapidly excluded from work as cowboys in the West.

15. T F Even the end of Reconstruction did not at first prevent African Americans from voting; some states continued to elect black legislators into the 1890s.

16. T F Utah was admitted as a state in 1896, after the Mormon Church's president and council banned polygamy, declaring their intention to submit to the laws of the United States.

17. T F In 1877 the Supreme Court ruled that neither states nor Congress had any constitutional authority to regulate rates charged by railroads.

18. T F From 1877 to 1890, national politics reflected a balance of power between East, West, and South, Democrats and Republicans, and among the three branches of government.

19. T F Harsh weather in the late 1880s devastated western cattle herds and forced consolidation in ranching.

## G. MULTIPLE CHOICE—circle one or more correct answers.

1. Which of these statements concerning racial relations in the United States in the late nineteenth century would be true?
   a) African Americans quickly came to be considered as equal to white Americans, while American Indians were treated as a distinct and inferior race.
   b) African Americans sought full integration into American society, only to be rejected.
   c) American Indians quickly came to be considered as culturally equal to white Americans, while African Americans were treated as a distinct and inferior race.
   d) Many Americans of European ancestry romanticized American Indians as brave and honorable children of the forest.
   e) Federal policy and some private institutions attempted to assimilate American Indians, most of whom spurned the offer.

2. The United States fought in 1876 and 1877 to take control of the Black Hills
   a) despite a treaty signed in 1868 guaranteeing the area to the Lakota.
   b) after Chief Red Cloud threatened to drive all whites into the Atlantic Ocean.
   c) because wagon trains traveling through Kansas were being raided.
   d) because gold had been discovered in the hills.
   e) in order to establish a national park and preserve the region's natural beauty.

3. In the presidential election of 1876,
   a) Republican Rutherford B. Hayes won an overwhelming popular vote majority.
   b) the Electoral College vote was close and the popular vote in several states disputed.
   c) a special commission split its vote along party lines.

d) southern Democrats finally acquiesced in yielding the presidency to a Republican who agreed to end Reconstruction.
e) African American voters supported the Democratic Party in large numbers.

4. During the nationwide railroad strike of 1877,
   a) railway craft brotherhoods called for an immediate socialist revolution.
   b) rail companies agreed that large wage increases were needed to keep the peace.
   c) state authorities sent militia units against strikers.
   d) the American Federation of Labor emerged to lead open class struggle.
   e) President Hayes called out federal troops to put an end to the strike.

5. The energies that drove manufacturing from the early nineteenth century to late century
   a) changed very little, coming from the heat in gigantic coal furnaces.
   b) came at first from water power.
   c) were derived from Irish laborers in the North and slaves sold to industrial enterprises in the South, both groups keeping complex gear systems turning.
   d) for a time switched from water to steam.
   e) slowly began to draw on electricity, which made possible the powering of extensive rows of machines and, in time, assembly lines.

6. The term "free market" in nineteenth-century labor took its meaning from a capitalist system
   a) that southern slave-owning critics attacked for being "wage slavery."
   b) that provided most families of the period with opportunities to own their own homes and take frequent leisure time.
   c) allowing employers to hold wages down, keep hours long, and take no responsibility for workers' health or safety.
   d) in which labor was bought and sold as one more commodity, to be priced and disposed of according to the whims of the market.
   e) that provided prosperity to freed slaves and newly arriving immigrants through stable jobs at substantial wages.

7. Which of these statements would apply to economic conditions in the United States in the nineteenth century?
   a) Throughout the century, most immigrant workers could supplement their wages with the sale of produce from land.
   b) At first, because cheap land was easy to get, hiring labor required good wages.
   c) Workers were paid little because Puritan capitalists kept the land to themselves.
   d) After the Civil War, employers in much of the country could draw on a pool of unemployed labor that kept down wages.
   e) Rising land prices fueled a general prosperity for most immigrant families.

8. The Knights of Labor, organized in 1869 in Philadelphia, Pennsylvania,
   a) concentrated on organizing skilled workers, putting them into craft guilds similar to the guilds of medieval times.
   b) built clandestine strike forces to engage in sabotage and intimidation.
   c) drew in African Americans, women, immigrants, and unskilled workers.
   d) adopted the form of a fraternal organization common in the country at that time.
   e) sought labor ownership through cooperatives of railroads, mines, and factories.

9. A bomb was thrown at police in Haymarket Square in Chicago, May 4, 1886,
   a) during a labor rally.
   b) to protest brutality toward African American and Puerto Rican residents.
   c) after several days of clashes between protesters and police.

d) for which several anarchists were tried, but released on a technicality.

e) and in the aftermath employers and authorities carried on a general attack on unions and labor activism across the country.

10. The culture of Plains Indians in the eighteenth century and the nineteenth depended on
a) selling gold from the Black Hills to obtain trade goods.
b) horses, acquired after Europeans imported the animals to America.
c) bison, which supplied meat, skins, and sinews.
d) banding with immigrant and ethnic minorities throughout North America.
e) chips of dried bison droppings to provide fuel for cooking fires.

11. Immigrants entering the United States at the turn of the twentieth century
a) came in large numbers from southern and eastern Europe, with slightly darker skin than the Americans of British or northern European stock who dominated political, social, and economic life.
b) in the western states arrived from Mexico and Japan.
a) were relatively poor, knew only scraps of English, and were widely thought to be ill fitted to adapt to life in the United States.
c) were in most cases Roman Catholic or Jewish, and therefore outside what many Americans thought to be the Protestant character of the nation.
d) ended up, in both city and country, living in racial or ethnic ghettoes.

12. Transcontinental rail lines that tied the country together after 1869 included
a) the Union Pacific and Central Pacific, joined in Utah.
b) the Great Atlantic and Pacific, carrying Chinese tea to New York.
c) the Southern Pacific.
d) the Northern Pacific and Great Northern lines.
e) the Western Rail Express Road's track through Utah to northern California.

13. Debate over whether gold should be supplemented by silver as the main basis of currency
a) pitted wealthy capitalists against organized labor.
b) divided creditors, who favored a stable gold currency, against debtors, who would prefer to repay their debts in money backed by devalued silver.
c) drew farmers and silver miners together in support of silver currency.
d) empowered Farmers' Alliances and propelled the new Populist Party.

14. The symbolic closing of the frontier in 1890 marked not so much the density of population on the land of the United States as
a) a tilt in agriculture from subsistence farming to market farming of commodities for sale.
b) the increased number of American millionaires seeking adventurous hunting grounds overseas rather than in the western territories.
c) an increase in the use of farm machinery.
d) construction of luxury log cabin lodges for tourists in national parks.

15. Texas cattle drives and the open range grazing system came to an end because
a) too many armed bands were rustling cattle on the trail north.
b) on the trail the cattle lost weight, and the railroads provided access to shipping points.
c) environmental regulations barred cattle herds from drinking water.
d) farmers, sheepherders, and cattle ranchers themselves were invading the open range.
e) huge nature preserves for bison left no grass for cattle to eat.

## H. ESSAY QUESTIONS OR ORAL REPORTS

1. Study the emergence of any one industry in the United States after the Civil War, or the concentration of an existing industry into fewer hands. Look up available data as to the real impact on the lives of most American families. (There is eloquent propaganda available from all sides

on the unsurpassed benefits or horrible disasters inflicted by industrial monopolies during this time.) Include information on actual changes in the industry of your choice, such as sources of power, methods of production, or patterns of employment.

2. Compare the suppression of the 1877 railroad strike with the withdrawal of federal troops from former Confederate states in the same year. What interests in government, industry, and the general civilian population supported each measure? Who was opposed? Did the two measures have the support of the same groups, or draw on the same arguments? Can you propose different policies which would have been healthier for democracy and economic growth?

3. Analyze the history of importation and exclusion of Chinese laborers. What companies, industries, and regions relied in part on Chinese labor? For what reasons did the presence of Chinese become unpopular? Who instigated and led anti-Chinese riots? What life did this leave for Chinese already in the United States?

4. Read additional sources on the history of the Knights of Labor, the American Federation of Labor, or both. Prepare a summary of the strengths and weaknesses of either, or compare the strengths and weaknesses of both. How did the one or two organizations of your choosing benefit or harm the general public outside the organization itself? Looking backward, can you define a strategy for labor that would have produced better results for workers and their families? For the nation as a whole?

5. Picking any one Indian people, document the manner in which traditional Indian customs continued in practice on reservations, and the real impact of the General Allotment Act. Of the Native Americans you have chosen, how did that act improve or destroy their ability to support themselves? What policy could have better maintained peace while allowing the Indians to thrive? Why was the policy you propose not adopted at the time?

6. Prepare a summary of the flight of the Nez Percé, treating its actions as an extended military operation. Analyze the tactics and strategy of the Indians and their pursuers. Include supply lines or other sources of goods, along with logistics, means of transportation, and the impact of terrain.

_____

_____

_____

_____

_____

_____

_____

_____

_____

_____

_____

_____

_____

_____

_____

_____

_____

# The Search for New Frontiers  17

## A. TERMS

National Forest _____

_____

_____

investment bankers _____

_____

_____

trust _____

_____

_____

holding company _____

_____

_____

Pinkertons _____

_____

_____

safety valve _____

_____

_____

alternating current _____

_____

_____

## B. PHOTOGRAPHS

1. If you were a capitalist, and you knew of L. Frank Baum's Populist viewpoint, how would you rewrite the script for *The Wizard of Oz* (picture on next page) to uphold the sanctity of private property and warn against the danger of mob rule?

_____

_____

_____

_____

_____
_____
_____
_____
_____
_____
_____
_____
_____
_____
_____
_____
_____
_____
_____
_____

2.  Find three features on the cover on the next page that represent a style or theme in advertising markedly different from the ways businesses today present themselves to the public, and find three similarities. There is no "right answer," as long as your facts are accurate; each person will notice or pay attention to different features of commerce.

_____
_____
_____
_____
_____
_____
_____

## C. VOCABULARY

scabs _____

_____

solidarity _____

_____

"sweater" (not the article of clothing) _____

_____

lynching _____

_____

Jim Crow _____

_____

_____

socialism _____

_____

_____

smelt _____

_____

_____

dysentery _____

_____

_____

## D. INDIVIDUALS

Thomas Edison _____

_____

_____

Frederick Jackson Turner _____

_____

_____

Marcus Daly _____

_____

_____

John D. Rockefeller _____

_____

_____

Alexander Graham Bell _____

_____

_____

Gustavus Swift _____

_____

_____

George Westinghouse _____

_____

_____

Henry Bessemer _____

_____

_____

Henry George _____

_____

_____

NAME _____ DATE _____

Henry Flagler _____
_____

James McParlan _____
_____

Andrew Carnegie _____
_____

Henry Clay Frick _____
_____

Karl Marx _____
_____

J. P. Morgan _____
_____

Horatio Alger _____
_____

John Peter Altgeld _____
_____

Jane Addams _____
_____

Ida Wells-Barnett _____
_____

Edward Bellamy _____
_____

James Baird Weaver _____
_____

Tom Watson _____
_____

43

"Sockless Jerry" Simpson _____

_____

_____

Grover Cleveland _____

_____

_____

Mary Elizabeth Lease _____

_____

_____

Jacob Coxey _____

_____

_____

William Jennings Bryan _____

_____

_____

William McKinley _____

_____

_____

## E. TRUE FALSE—circle one.

1. T F Steel was of little industrial use until new processes to burn off excess carbon and impurities made it essential for construction girders.
2. T F Stuck in the heat and humidity of Florida waiting for duty in the Spanish-American War, white soldiers made friends with the state's African American population.
3. T F During the 1892 strike against Carnegie's Homestead steel mill, a member of the Pennsylvania militia was court-martialed for proposing "three cheers for the man who shot Frick," Carnegie's union-busting general manager.
4. T F In 1900, about two-thirds of Americans were self-employed, while the remaining minority found jobs as wage earners.
5. T F At the turn of the twentieth century, children between ten and fifteen years old held about 700,000 jobs outside the farm, working in coalfields or textile mills or shining shoes and running errands.
6. T F People's Party leaders consistently demanded that all African Americans should be denied any participation in elections, and prohibited from owning land.
7. T F Populist candidates failed to carry the electoral votes of a single state in any presidential election, because voters pragmatically stuck with the Democrats and Republicans.
8. T F Jacob Coxey's vision was for a federal program of road building that would put the unemployed to work and send currency through the depressed economy.
9. T F After the Supreme Court decision in *Plessy* v. *Ferguson*, the federal government vigorously enforced the ruling that segregated facilities for black Americans must be equal facilities to whites.
10. T F After 1880 refrigeration technology was sufficiently well developed to allow for year-round shipment of meat.
11. T F Aiming to make a huge profit from the rise in the price of gold, Jay Gould spread a rumor the government was going to buy gold. The subsequent crash in the gold market created a panic on Wall Street.
12. T F Thousands of women who worked at home as seamstresses for outside employers were not counted in the 1880 census as working women.

13. T F Although conglomerates of industry and finance wielded great power, individual isolated farmers by their sheer numbers dictated rates and prices.
14. T F Coxey's Army, or the Army of the Commonweal, brought so many people to Washington that President Cleveland believed that the government might fall.
15. T F As Chicago's population and industry grew in the 1890s, landlords divided suburban single-family homes on the West Side into four or five apartments each.
16. T F Socialist electoral gains reached their peak in 1912 when Eugene Debs received 900,000 votes for president, while some socialists were elected mayors and state legislators.
17. T F President William McKinley, who presided over acquisition of Cuba, Puerto Rico, and the Philippines, was a staunch advocate of free trade.

## F. MULTIPLE CHOICE—circle one or more correct answers.

1. The Columbian Exposition in Chicago in 1893
    a) commemorated the hundredth anniversary of Colombia's independence from Spain.
    b) employed a quarter million workers to construct over two hundred million square feet of buildings.
    c) focused on commemoration of the vanishing American frontier.
    d) received over twenty-seven million visitors, about one fourth of the nation's population.
    e) presented a spacious city demonstrating the forces of science and industry.

2. Successful capitalists of the Gilded Age obtained their fortunes from
    a) a combination of luck and business skill in using new technologies.
    b) saving money one dollar at a time from low-paid jobs, then investing it in modest but steady savings accounts.
    c) pilfering charitable funds intended for widows and orphans.
    d) the hard work of millions of employees whose unions they were prepared to break.
    e) politics and a corrupt economy.

3. By 1880, women working outside the home
    a) amounted to only about one percent of the paid labor force.
    b) made up sixty percent of public-school teachers.
    c) found most clerical positions closed to them.
    d) moved into sales jobs as well as nursing and social work.
    e) had no place in the legal profession, but a few hundred had become doctors.

4. Prejudice against Hispanics in territories taken from Mexico was
    a) eased by friendly business deals between established residents and newly arriving Anglos.
    b) restrained by equitable resolution of land claims brought before the Board of Land Commissioners in California.
    c) sharpened due to increased land ownership by the many *mexicanos* and *californios*, while Anglo settlers believed that all the land was waiting for Anglos to occupy it.
    d) tempered by the protection of the Texas Rangers against land-grabbing settlers, and favorable tax laws.
    e) intensified by adherence to the Roman Catholic faith, which the largely Protestant population of the United States distrusted.

5. The program of the People's Party (Populists) called for
    a) cheap currency based on coinage of silver to replace the gold standard.
    b) banning women from the workplace and restricting the vote to white males.
    c) ejection of anyone who questioned the wisdom of war to which the United States army had been committed.
    d) government ownership of railroads, telegraphs, and telephone systems.
    e) a system of government warehouses where farmers could store their crop and receive credit for it, until it could be sold at the best price.

6. Between 1873 and 1900 American technology added
    a) pocket pagers.            b) desktop computers.            c) typewriters.
    d) phonographs.              e) telephones.

7. The opening of department stores changed retail business in the following ways:
    a) Most departments were reserved for wealthy customers, who no longer had to mix with the lower classes to shop.
    b) Some stores were large enough to have separate black and white departments for each kind of article offered for sale.
    c) The ancient customs of haggling and bargaining were replaced with a uniform price for each item.
    d) They commanded high enough volume to persuade manufacturers it was good business to sell at low rates, and the stores could accordingly lower their own prices.
    e) They drove out of business traditional five and dime stores like Woolworth's.

8. Hazards of work at the close of the nineteenth century included
    a) industrial accidents that in an average year killed about 35,000 Americans.
    b) sudden thunderstorms that electrocuted twenty-five farm workers every week.
    c) gas fires in mines that could scorch a worker's lungs.
    d) stab wounds from angry fellow employees that wounded 53,000 a year.
    e) tuberculosis that resulted from overcrowding, malnutrition, and weakness from overwork.

9. Women working at home doing contract clothing work for large companies
    a) enjoyed good health that direct employment and the use of steam power would have destroyed.
    b) suffered chronic injury from repetitive use of foot-powered sewing machines.
    c) in most cases froze to death within two or three winters of beginning work.
    d) contracted respiratory congestion from buckets of dye stored in their kitchens.

10. Among the resources provided by Jane Addams at Hull House were
    a) kindergarten and day care for children of the ward's working mothers.
    b) a library and classrooms for music and art programs for children and adults.
    c) a cooperative residence for working women.
    d) a Labor Museum and community theater productions.
    e) job information for laborers seeking employment.

11. A riot and lynching in Memphis, Tennessee, in 1892 was the result of
    a) a rumor that three black men had raped five white women.
    b) anger by whites at the objections a black laborer raised at the mistreatment of his wife.
    c) resentment by white grocery store owners toward a black-owned grocery that competed with them.
    d) resentment on the part of drunken unemployed white men that employers preferred to hire hard-working black laborers.
    e) anger that three black co-owners of a grocery store, attacked by a mob, fought back, wounding three whites.

12. Indian students sent to the Carlisle School in Pennsylvania
    a) were given pre-frontal lobotomies so they would forget their Indian identity.
    b) received haircuts and Euro-American clothing immediately upon arrival.
    c) welcomed the respectful multicultural curriculum at the school.
    d) lived under regulations requiring them to speak only in English.
    e) grew their hair long and returned to Indian identities upon graduation.

13. A wide variety of socialist thought included
    a) a conviction that machinery robs its operators of independence, and capitalist owners complete their enslavement.
    b) a hope among some radicals that modern technology refines the act of work, and requires new levels of intelligence on the part of the workforce.

c) a call to inspiring workers to fight for a future in which they would be automatons who could relax their minds as the machinery does the work.

d) conflicting hopes for violent revolution or peaceful resolution of class struggles.

e) forms of Christian socialism drawing on religious faith and principles.

14. In many areas of the Great Plains and Rocky Mountains, the Homestead Act of 1862

a) provided that one square mile out of every sixteen should be reserved for the support of Indian tribes who agreed to live under the rule of the United States.

b) reflected ignorance of the country to be claimed, offering 160-acre homesteads when many regions required dry farming drawing on 640-acres or more.

c) emptied New York of Jewish immigrants, who preferred to make their living by farming as they had done in Russia and Poland.

d) contained farsighted provisions for sustainable forestry and scientific management of watersheds.

e) was used to obtain land at $1.25 an acre by individuals who resold it to large ranchers or corporations seeking to expand their landholdings.

## G. ESSAY QUESTIONS OR ORAL REPORTS

1. Examine the wording of at least three late nineteenth-century United States Supreme Court decisions concerning state and federal regulation of business and industry. What constitutional principles underlie these decisions? What practical considerations and interest groups also had an influence?

2. Study the career of Mark Hanna, the preeminent Republican Party boss at the turn of the last century. What principles motivated his choices? How would you square with the common view of Hanna as a reactionary with the complex presentation offered by Charles W. Bailey (www.cosmos-club.orgjournals/1997/bailey.html)? How did his style and work differ from that of the Tammany Hall machine in New York's Democratic Party? Why did he despise Theodore Roosevelt?

3. Analyze the Supreme Court decision in *Plessy* v. *Ferguson* (see www.brandywinesources.com) for the constitutional principles it invoked, and the facts of the specific dispute brought to the court. For example, Plessy's first objection was that he looked white, so the state had no business calling him Negro. How did the court deal with that? What principles do you find in Justice Harlan's dissent? What references made by Justice Harlan would, by modern standards, be considered unacceptable by the majority? In conclusion, summarize the practical significance of this case for American law.

4. Develop a chronology of the major nineteenth-century discoveries that brought about today's system of electrical power: generation itself, alternating as opposed to direct current, long-distance transmission, methods of storage.

5. Select and analyze one of the major strikes of the Gilded Age, including the Homestead Steel strike, the Coeur d'Alene miners' strike, or the Pullman railroad strike. Detail the interests that motivated management and union, the tactics and strategies of each, and the role played by local, state, and federal governments. Suggest ways the union might have gotten a better result with different tactics or strategies, and ways that with a different approach management might have secured a more productive work environment.

6. Consider socialism in the United States in the late nineteenth century, bearing in mind both changes in the nation's economic life and the ideas brought by immigrants. Why did defenders of laissez-faire capitalism and advocates of working-class organizations both speak of "freedom"?

7. Report on land use patterns as they actually developed in the Great Plains and Rocky Mountain states in the late nineteenth century. Take into consideration the intent of the Homestead Act of 1862, the Timber and Stone Act of 1878, and the General Land Law Revision Act of 1891. Document how land use actually developed in spite of these laws. Explain both natural conditions that forced a different pattern of development and actions by people who took what the law did not provide for.

8. Look into the individual leaders and the geographic and demographic constituencies contributing to the People's Party. How did all agree on a common program? In what different directions did these various subgroups drift in later years? To what parties, programs, philosophies, and practices did they give their loyalty? Since this is a large subject for one essay: either give a brief overview of the entire picture, or focus in detail on a small number of individuals and constituencies.

9. Select a major industry that emerged in the United States between 1877 and 1900. Write an account of its origins, including technological advances, individual investment decisions, demographic opportunities, and natural resources available.

# Taming the Forces of Social Change

## 18

## A. TERMS

One Big Union _____
_____
_____

progressivism _____
_____
_____

Triangle Shirtwaist fire _____
_____
_____

Ludlow Massacre _____
_____
_____

New Immigrants _____
_____
_____

melting pot _____
_____
_____

*Bintel Brief* _____
_____
_____

Social Gospel _____
_____
_____

*Rerum novarum* _____
_____
_____

Niagara Movement _____
_____
_____

muckrakers _____

_____

_____

scientific management _____

_____

_____

Social Darwinism _____

_____

_____

Ashcan School _____

_____

_____

## B. PHOTOGRAPHS

1. Louis Sullivan was known during his lifetime for bringing clean modern form to buildings, which he achieved by the use of steel reinforcements. What in this building seems to you most modern? Or do you see it as cluttered and busy rather than relatively spare and lean? Do you see both clutter and leanness? In any case, point to features that back up your argument. Do not be hindered by your lack of architectural training. Sullivan meant his buildings to be viewed by a wide public rather than a handful of the artistically schooled.

_____

_____

_____

_____

_____

_____

_____

_____

_____

_____

_____

_____

_____

_____

_____

_____

_____

_____

_____

_____

_____

_____

_____

_____

_____

_____

_____

_____

_____

_____

_____

_____

_____

_____

_____

_____

_____

2. These immigrants may be waiting for the frightening process of inspection, or they may be looking to their future in the New World. Suggest what might have been their thoughts and feelings at the moment. Would dread, eagerness, or curiosity be mingled, or would one of these dominate? Going on either of two common but conflicting assumptions about children—that they are more equipped for adventure or that their usual emotions are fear and insecurity—decide who in this group might be most or least prepared to step into a new country.

_____
_____
_____
_____
_____
_____
_____
_____
_____
_____

3. This moment of Hester Street life in New York City could be described, perhaps condescendingly, as crammed and disordered, a pressing together of immigrants lacking the means of a more neatly arranged existence. Or it could be described, perhaps sentimentally, as a cheerful scene of people who are well adjusted to what they are doing and going about it efficiently. Find details that will justify either interpretation or both.

_____
_____
_____
_____
_____
_____
_____
_____
_____
_____
_____
_____
_____
_____
_____
_____
_____
_____
_____
_____

_____
_____
_____

_____
_____
_____
_____
_____
_____
_____
_____
_____
_____
_____
_____
_____
_____
_____
_____

**4.** This lynching is separated from the present by a century at most. Yet today no expression of racial dominance and cruelty so blatant could be expected to take place in this country and be photographed (television news stories warn viewers of any unpleasant scene about to be presented). Does the photo suggest that the morality and sensitivity of the nation were different at the time: that brutality of this kind may have been more casually present even in matters unconnected with race? Or do you think that racial hatred this great could have existed in isolation from the rest of American culture and society? Justify your conclusion by whatever you know of the time and any facts of present-day American culture you think relevant.

_____
_____
_____
_____
_____
_____
_____
_____
_____
_____
_____
_____
_____
_____

## C. VOCABULARY

Wobbly _____
_____
_____

sabotage _____
_____
_____

Chautauqua _____
_____
_____

Yiddish _____
_____
_____

*padrone* system _____
_____
_____

pragmatism _____
_____
_____

## D. INDIVIDUALS

Elizabeth Gurley Flynn _____
_____
_____

William "Big Bill" Haywood _____
_____
_____

**NAME** _____ **DATE** _____

Samuel Gompers _____
_____

Samuel M. "Golden Rule" Jones _____
_____

Tom Johnson _____
_____

Alfred E. Smith _____
_____

Louis Sullivan _____
_____

Dennis Kearney _____
_____

Abraham Cahan _____
_____

Israel Zangwill _____
_____

Washington Gladden _____
_____

Walter Rauschenbusch _____
_____

Frances Willard _____
_____

Florence Kelley _____
_____

Alice Hamilton _____
_____

Margaret Sanger _____

_____

_____

Booker T. Washington _____

_____

_____

Ida Tarbell _____

_____

_____

Lincoln Steffens _____

_____

_____

Frederick Winslow Taylor _____

_____

_____

Thorstein Veblen _____

_____

_____

D. W. Griffith _____

_____

_____

William James _____

_____

_____

John Dewey _____

_____

_____

Oliver Wendell Holmes, Jr. _____

_____

_____

Alfred Stieglitz _____

_____

_____

Jacob Riis _____

_____

_____

Stephen Crane _____

_____

_____

Frank Norris _____
_____
_____

## E. ORGANIZATIONS

Industrial Workers of the World (IWW) _____
_____
_____

International Ladies' Garment Workers Union (ILGWU) _____
_____
_____

Women's Christian Temperance Union (WCTU) _____
_____
_____

National Association for the Advancement of Colored People (NAACP) _____
_____
_____

Society of American Indians _____
_____
_____

League of United Latin American Citizens (LULAC) _____
_____
_____

## F. TRUE FALSE—circle one.

1. T F The IWW wanted a more aggressive recruitment of skilled and highly paid workers than the AFL was willing to conduct.
2. T F In organizing Philadelphia longshoremen after the end of the First World War, the AFL broke with its usual policy of avoiding the recruitment of black workers.
3. T F Among the uses of the word "progressivism" in reference to movements at the turn of the twentieth century is its employment in identifying efforts to bring trained expertise to the management of industrial forces.
4. T F The Ludlow Massacre led to state laws crafted by Alfred E. Smith and Robert Wagner governing factory conditions.
5. T F Crowding in Chicago at the turn of the twentieth century was worsened by the city's reliance on old horse-drawn means of public transportation.
6. T F Immigration was driven mostly by the unbearable misery of the migrants in their homelands.
7. T F Members of the staffs of settlement houses had to adapt their middle-class behavior to the manners of their immigrant clientele.
8. T F Progressive reformers believed that consolidation in industry and other institutions was inevitably corruptive of social health.
9. T F Like more recent libertarian radicals who embrace forms of social liberation, followers of the Social Gospel defended the liquor trade.

10. T  F  In their criticism of the double standard that allowed men a freer sexual experience than women, some progressive reformers called for an equally free sexual life for both genders while most doubtless wanted both to abstain from sex outside of marriage.

11. T  F  Refusing to make any distinction among reasons for borrowing, critics of the lending trade wanted every transaction to be paid for from the earned or inherited funds of the purchaser.

12. T  F  Immigrant peddlers acting for enterprises conducting installment plans were able to help newcomers learn about the workings of retail buying.

13. T  F  Progressive reformers paid little notice to prostitution, believing it to be a private affair between suppliers and clients.

14. T  F  Progressive reformers thought to rescue borrowers from both the injustices of unscrupulous lenders and the recklessness of the borrowers themselves.

15. T  F  The promotion of model lending laws met with universal resistance from illegal lenders.

16. T  F  Booker T. Washington and W. E. B. Du Bois disagreed over what kind of schooling, practical or liberal arts, would most promote among students a character fit for survival in American society.

17. T  F  The activism that expressed itself in the NAACP had no parallel among American Indians and citizens of Latin American origin.

18. T  F  Among the three hundred thousand students attending colleges and universities at the turn of the twentieth century, women constituted about one percent.

19. T  F  In the late nineteenth century, about nine in ten Americans were classifiable as literate.

20. T  F  A possible reason for D. W. Griffith's screening of *Intolerance* was to dispel the image of racist hate-monger he had gotten from *Birth of a Nation.*

21. T  F  Factory workers had no ability to resist on the job the pace of work set by management.

22. T  F  Social Darwinists were mistaken in thinking that biologists placed competition among individuals at the basis of evolution.

23. T  F  William James insisted that everyday experience muddies thought and is the enemy of truth, which is to be found only in a rigorous process of logical meditation.

## G. MULTIPLE CHOICE—circle one or more correct answers.

1. The strategy of the IWW included
   a) acts of sabotage.
   b) persuading employers that good wages and reasonable hours would make for a healthier and more efficient workforce.
   c) demanding that the federal government establish mechanisms for resolution of industrial disputes.
   d) acts of rebellion in which the worker would be at once taking possession of freedom and aiding in the overthrow of capitalism.
   e) organizing textile workers in Lawrence, Massachusetts.

2. Chicago was marked by
   a) the variety of its industries.
   b) its maintenance of a population largely Anglo-American in contrast to the immigrant communities in other cities.
   c) its laws requiring that buildings be constructed only of brick or stone, materials safe from fire.
   d) a pattern of settlement in which successive waves of immigrants would take over neighborhoods abandoned by prospering older groups that moved on.
   e) an outward sprawl as industries and population sought new space in which to locate.

3. Great shifts in population at the turn of the century
   a) involved immigration to the United States but also migrations within countries as well as from one European nation to another.
   b) was generally from the cities to the countryside.
   c) for the most part sent to this country migrants from the same parts of Europe as had come in earlier waves.
   d) brought customs that charmed Americans of older stock for their quaintness and color.
   e) took place amid much distrust among the migrants toward the officials they dealt with.

4. In seeking forms of work,
   a) Jews quickly abandoned their determination to respect their religion's Sabbath as a day of rest.
   b) many Slavic workers took to mining.
   c) Chinese on the West Coast received aid from the Workingmen's Party.
   d) Scottish immigrants were served by a *padrone* system of bosses who connected workers to jobs.
   e) many Slavs as well as Japanese planned to make enough to take back to their homeland.

5. For their housing, many New Immigrants
   a) in New York City lived in tenements suggestive of dumb-bells, the apartments placed on two sides of a central airshaft.
   b) seeking to increase their scanty incomes took lodgers into apartments already crowded.
   c) hid from the authorities miserable conditions that violated the law, for they feared eviction.
   d) were able by political pressure to force contractors to put up apartments that were supposed to relieve crowding.

6. In their adjustment to their new land,
   a) Jewish immigrants had good contacts with the Irish police, some of whom learned a bit of Yiddish or wore Jewish luck tokens.
   b) New Immigrants had to fend off the hostility of New York City's Tammany Hall.
   c) New Immigrants had little help from the AFL.
   d) new waves of Mexicans in the Southwest could find common cause with the descendants of earlier migrants from Mexico.
   e) Italians, Japanese, and Chinese lacked the ability earlier immigrants had shown to organize societies for mutual support.

7. In the contact of immigrant culture with American ways,
   a) dance halls could have introduced young girls to a more open social life than their immigrant parents.
   b) the public schools got the confidence of immigrant parents for the ease with which they reconciled immigrant with American culture.
   c) Educational Alliances formed by German Jews of older immigration seemed at times condescending toward East European Jews, yet aided their adjustment to their new home.
   d) many children of New Immigrants seemed to their parents overly eager to become Anglicized to the abandonment of the old customs.
   e) Abraham Cahan argued that for their protection, Jewish immigrants should withdraw into their own culture in face of an environment determined to be hostile to them.

8. Among attempts to find a Christian response to industrial conditions,
   a) the Social Gospel preached that the divine Kingdom can have no fruitful contact with earthly institutions, which inevitably soil the virtue of good Christians.
   b) the Social Gospel preached that even such worldly reforms as factory legislation would aid in the coming of the Kingdom.
   c) the National Council of Churches was organized by more traditional Christians opposed to the Social Gospel.
   d) *Rerum novarum* was an effort on the part of Pope Leo XIII to reconcile the Roman Catholic Church with the social and political forces of his age.
   e) *Rerum novarum*, urging capitalists to resist any compromise with labor, argued that compromise would amount to a sinful abandonment of the rights of private property taught by the Church.

9. Among women professionals and reformers,
   a) Frances Willard of the Women's Christian Temperance Union argued that alcohol was promoted by labor radicals and constituted an evidence of the evil of radicalism.
   b) alcohol was defined as particularly a women's concern, for women and their children are the victims of male drunkenness.

c) Florence Kelley aided in the passage of Illinois legislation regulating the working conditions of women and children.

d) advocates of a larger role for women had to confront the notion that their gender was by nature too frail to enter the rough realm of politics and reform.

e) settlement houses provided an inspiration and entrance to reform activity.

10. Among forms of reading and entertainment,

a) sensationalist papers known as yellow journals furnished much of the newspaper fare for Americans.

b) Yiddish, once scorned among educated Jews as inferior to German or Russian, came to maturity as a serious literary language.

c) some publications of light and racy stories were so full of sex and violence that their authors were known as muckrakers for the muck they dredged up.

d) movies remained in 1915 just what they had been in their earliest days, presenting brief and amusing stories and sought out only as interesting mechanical novelties.

e) the Chautauqua programs brought lectures in serious subjects to rural communities that lacked quick access to urban institutions.

11. Among social theorists who addressed industrial conditions,

a) Frederick Winslow Taylor proposed that for the sake of a system more productive in the long term, factories be dismantled and workers set to doing the old crafts at their own pace.

b) Thorstein Veblen argued that modern technology cultivates a taste for workmanlike efficiency, and should be run not by business concerned only with profits but by technicians who will allow workers to achieve satisfaction in their work.

c) Social Darwinists argued that competition, which they believed that science had found to be the source of evolution in nature, should be similarly placed at the center of economic life.

d) John Dewey urged that students be taught through activities that would give life to the ideas they were learning.

e) Oliver Wendell Holmes, Jr., insisted that legal reasoning should proceed by a method of pure logic with no reference to the practical intentions of citizens.

12. Among the contributors to artistic life at the turn of the century,

a) photographers offered their art, not quite accurately, as a way of capturing their surroundings with strict objectivity.

b) the Ashcan School of painters sought to achieve abstract interpretations of common scenes and objects.

c) John Marin in his painting of the Brooklyn Bridge broke with the Ashcan School, and captured the bridge in the matter-of-fact way that a common observer might see it.

d) Stephen Crane in *The Red Badge of Courage* portrays a Union soldier whose biological drives of fear and aggression end by overwhelming any element of reason and self-knowledge.

e) Frank Norris in *The Octopus* portrays a nature that begins as apparently disordered but ends by proving itself a giver of life and unity.

## H. ESSAY QUESTIONS OR ORAL REPORTS

1. Pick any one immigrant group as of the early twentieth century or just before. Draw on whatever immigrant ancestry you have that is applicable, or on your own experience if you were born abroad. Look up where a sampling of your chosen immigrants settled, what kinds of neighborhoods they formed, what work they sought, what they had in the way of religion and culture, and whether they had any distinctive politics or involvement in a labor movement. How did they go about forming communities and private lives, preserving old customs and assimilating the dominant ways of American society?

2. During the early twentieth century, reform movements had perhaps a greater willingness than today to ask fundamental questions about what society and even personal conduct should be all

about. Choose among any three of these: the Social Gospel, the Niagara Movement and its outgrowth in the NAACP, scientific management, Thorstein Veblen, Social Darwinism, and the legal theory of Oliver Wendell Holmes, Jr. Discuss what was similar among your three and what differed in the way they defined the good life, personal conduct, and the obstacles to the achievement of a good society.

3. Some historians are inclined to describe American history as a history of prejudice, and as a story of the dominance that this or that racial or ethnic group has exercised over another. Early in the twentieth century, the presence of the so-named New Immigrants awakened much cultural fear among Americans of longer ancestry in this country, along with partial exclusion from the established labor movement. It was also a time of newly invigorated activity among prominent black and in some cases white Americans in protest against racism and its social effects. In what ways can the experience of the New Immigrants be likened to that of African Americans of the period in economic conditions, practical obstacles to success, and prejudice faced?

4. The period discussed by this chapter was notable in the degree to which, in contrast with women of earlier times, women made themselves visible in reform movements and in the professions and in college student enrollments. Consider a sampling of the female figures, organizations, and purposes of the time. Was there a distinctively female point of view, a particularly female set of concerns, a notably female method of going about their tasks?

5. Read *The Titan* by Theodore Dreiser, Stephen Crane's *Red Badge of Courage*, and *The Octopus* by Frank Norris. All three have been classed under the general heading of naturalism, which refers to a form of literature that sees human life and society as the expression of natural forces. Yet the three are remarkably different from one another. Write a critical essay that describes the similarities and the differences, and come to a judgment about the whole naturalist project in literature. Which of the three novels seems most powerful, and which the least?

# Progressive Empire and Progressive Reform

# 19

## A. TERMS

diplomatic corps _____
_____
_____

Great White Fleet _____
_____
_____

yellow journalism _____
_____
_____

Platt Amendment _____
_____
_____

Open Door policy _____
_____
_____

direct primaries _____
_____
_____

initiative _____
_____
_____

referendum _____
_____
_____

recall _____
_____
_____

Roosevelt Corollary _____
_____
_____

Dollar Diplomacy _____

_____

_____

## B. PHOTOGRAPHS

1. Considering the social climate of 1901, develop a brief summary of what might have been going through the mind of Washington and of Roosevelt at this dinner. Why are they dining alone, with no other guests? Why did the Democratic Party of that time think it a good move to print campaign buttons of this dinner, implying that Roosevelt favored "race mingling?"

2. Do the images on the next page show Uncle Sam moving American principles of liberty into the wider world? Or moving the United States into the imperial designs of the wider world? Around 1900 many prominent Americans took various positions on these questions. Taking into consideration all facts you can locate, develop your own answer.

A FAIR FIELD AND NO FAVOR.

UNCLE SAM: "I'm out for commerce, not conquest."

_____
_____
_____
_____
_____
_____
_____
_____
_____
_____
_____
_____
_____
_____
_____
_____
_____
_____
_____
_____
_____
_____
_____
_____

## C. VOCABULARY

conservation _____

_____

_____

wilderness _____

_____

_____

ambassador _____

_____

_____

annexation _____

_____

_____

isthmus _____

_____

_____

imperialism _____

_____

_____

jingoism _____

_____

_____

## D. INDIVIDUALS

John Muir _____

_____

_____

Theodore Roosevelt _____

_____

_____

Gifford Pinchot _____

_____

_____

Alfred Thayer Mahan _____

_____

_____

Robert M. La Follette _____

_____

_____

John Hay _____

_____

_____

Porfirio Díaz _____

_____

_____

**E. MATCHING** Draw a line from the statement at left to the person who said it at right.

Coal miners "don't suffer, why, they can't even speak English."

"To hell with the Constitution when the people want coal."

Joe Cannon

"Roosevelt's got no more respect for the Constitution than a tomcat has for a marriage license."

John Muir

"Dam Hetch Hetchy! As well dam for water-tanks the people's cathedrals and churches."

Upton Sinclair

The principle of conservation is "to take every part of the land and its resources and put it to that use in which it will best serve the most people."

Theodore Roosevelt

George F. Baer

"There would be meat stored in great piles in rooms and the water from leaky roofs would drip over it, and thousands of rats would race about on it."

Gifford Pinchot

Put a checkmark beside reforms initiated and adopted during the administration of President Woodrow Wilson.

____ The Underwood Tariff lowering rates

____ The nation's first open housing law

____ The Clayton Anti-trust Act

____ The first federal minimum wage law

____ Aid to Families with Dependent Children

____ The Federal Farm Loan Act, providing loans to farmers at low interest rates

____ A workmen's compensation program for federal employees

____ Desegregation of the armed forces

____ Appointment of the first Securities and Exchange Commission

____ The Adamson Act, setting an eight-hour day for railroad workers

____ Extension of the vote to women in all elections

____ The Keating-Owen Act, forbidding interstate transportation of products of child labor

____ The Kellogg-Briand Pact outlawing war

**F. TRUE FALSE**—circle one.
1.  T   F   Plans to build a canal across Central America from the Atlantic to the Pacific focused at first on Nicaragua, which had a large lake and passage at sea level that would not require locks.
2.  T   F   In 1880, the United States navy ranked twelfth in the world; by 1900 the fleet ranked third.
3.  T   F   Documents released decades after the Spanish-American War, and careful reconstruction of accounts at the time, indicate that the battleship *Maine* was destroyed by accident.
4.  T   F   Of the 5,400 American soldiers who died during the Spanish-American War, about four hundred died of illness, and the rest of wounds sustained in combat.
5.  T   F   The Republican Party nominated Theodore Roosevelt for vice president in 1900 because party conservatives wanted the unpredictable Roosevelt out of New York State politics.

6.  T  F  Woodrow Wilson, like Theodore Roosevelt a believer in Anglo-Saxon superiority, criticized what he termed the mongrel races of southern and eastern Europe.

7.  T  F  In the 1890s the United States began exchanging ambassadors with foreign nations, instead of sending representatives with the humbler rank of minister.

8.  T  F  In 1900 American troops joined with a popular Chinese movement called the Righteous Fists to curtail European colonial exploitation of China.

9.  T  F  In 1900 the Democratic Party was the party of progressive reform, while the Republican Party refused to limit or criticize corporate wealth.

10.  T  F  After clashes between African American soldiers stationed at Brownsville, Texas, and local white civilians, Theodore Roosevelt dismissed all charges against members of three black companies.

11.  T  F  The Teller Amendment to the Spanish-American War resolution recognizing Cuban independence from Spain announced that the United States had no claim to control of the island.

12.  T  F  Filipino insurrectionists against Spain found they had to fight also against their American liberators.

13.  T  F  By 1901 one percent of all the industrial firms in the United States were producing almost half of the nation's manufactured goods.

14.  T  F  Theodore Roosevelt aided in negotiating an end to the Russo-Japanese War of 1904, essentially sealing a Japanese victory.

15.  T  F  President William Howard Taft sent troops to Honduras and Nicaragua to support political factions friendly to the business interests of the United States.

16.  T  F  The United States Supreme Court in 1918 found unconstitutional the Keating-Owen Act, prohibiting interstate transportation of products of child labor.

17.  T  F  In the presidential election of 1916, a majority of the Supreme Court threatened to rule that the Republican Charles Evans Hughes had won the election.

## G. MULTIPLE CHOICE—circle one or more correct answers.

1. From 1898 to 1899 the United States acquired these territories in the Pacific and Caribbean:
   a) the Dominican Republic and Midway.
   b) Hawaii, Wake Island, and Guam.
   c) Cuba, Haiti, and Honduras.
   d) Puerto Rico and the Philippines.
   e) Okinawa, the Marianas, and Formosa.

2. Events preceding construction of the Panama Canal included
   a) negotiations with the League of Nations to secure an international mandate for the United States to build and operate the canal.
   b) the Hay-Pauncefote Treaty, in which Britain gave the United States sole right to build and fortify a Central American canal, though it must remain open to use by other nations.
   c) a revolution in Panama to secede from Colombia, backed by a naval force from the United States, and aided by Colombian officers willing to surrender for money.
   d) liberation of Central America from Spanish colonial rule, so that the United States could negotiate a canal treaty with one of the newly independent nations.
   e) the Hay-Bunau-Varilla Treaty granting the United States a strip of territory to build the canal, in exchange for an initial payment and annual fees.

3. When Venezuela appealed to the United States for help in a boundary dispute with British Guiana,
   a) a division of United States marines was dispatched to secure the disputed territory.
   b) President Cleveland's administration tried to arbitrate, Britain rejected the effort, and Cleveland threatened resistance to any British intrusion.
   c) Britain and Venezuela accepted an offer to arbitrate the dispute.
   d) more concerned over rivalries with Germany, Britain agreed to an arbitration process that found mostly in favor of British claims.
   e) Venezuela and Britain fought a short undeclared war, which made only small changes in the disputed boundary, while the United States watched helplessly.

4. The Interstate Commerce Commission, under the Republican administrations of the early twentieth century, gained power to
   a) break up corporate property and turn it over to workers' cooperatives.
   b) set maximum railroad rates, and regulate telephone, cable, and telegraph companies.
   c) dissolve unions if it appeared their demands would bankrupt an employer.
   d) examine a railroad's books and prescribe accounting standards.
   e) forbid segregated seating on passenger trains crossing state lines.

5. American intervention in Cuba, which led Spain to declare war on the United States,
   a) resulted in complete and unrestricted independence for the island, which had been one of Spain's last colonial possessions in America.
   b) was motivated in part by public outrage over the Spanish practice of moving civilians into guarded camps to put down an insurrection for independence.
   c) became an even more powerful demand on the part of the public as journalists put out one theory after another about the destruction of the battleship *Maine* in Havana harbor.
   d) was motivated largely by a cold calculated desire on the part of businesses in the United States to take over the remnants of Spain's empire around the world.
   e) went against President McKinley's distaste for the war passions of the moment, but he eventually gave in to popular pressure.

6. Theodore Roosevelt gained a reputation for being a trustbuster because
   a) of his resolute refusal to approve the takeover of the Tennessee Coal and Iron Company by J. P. Morgan's United States Steel.
   b) his policies resulted in a drastic redistribution of the wealth of the United States to the advantage of the poor.
   c) he decided to prosecute J. P. Morgan's Northern Securities Trust as a monopoly outlawed by the Sherman Act.
   d) under his administration another forty-three more antitrust suits were filed.
   e) he rose to the presidency from an impoverished childhood.

7. Which of these were reasons for passing the nation's first Pure Food and Drug Law?
   a) Physicians and sellers of Coca Cola were widely promoting cocaine as a tonic and a curative for diseases.
   b) A liberal Democratic Party administration, backed by a large congressional majority, was blaming corporations for all the nation's ills.
   c) Gangs of drug dealers dominated the streets of major cities, but there was no law by which to prosecute their commerce or the accompanying violence.
   d) Grossly unsanitary conditions in the meatpacking industry, exposed by Upton Sinclair's novel *The Jungle*, had nauseated the public.
   e) J. P. Morgan's well-organized trusts stood to gain a great deal of profit on their investments if regulation drove competitors out of business.

8. The Roosevelt Corollary to the Monroe Doctrine
   a) announced that no European power could have any role in building a canal through Central America without the permission of the United States.
   b) was first announced after several European countries threatened to use military force to collect debts owed to them by various countries in the Americas.
   c) stipulated that Washington would act as an "international police power" in the event of "flagrant wrongdoing in the Western Hemisphere."
   d) recognized that as the history of European colonial domination faded, the nations of Latin America could take responsibility for their own sovereignty.
   e) gave an excuse for repeated interferences in Latin America whenever conditions there were not to the liking of the United States.

9. The Gentleman's Agreement worked out by President Roosevelt with Japan
   a) committed both governments to see that women of either nation were treated with courtesy and respect while visiting the other.
   b) persuaded the San Francisco school board to drop an order segregating Japanese and other Asian students.
   c) established that Japanese nationals in the United States would be treated as "white," while Chinese nationals would not.
   d) provided that Japan would restrict future immigration to the United States.
   e) provoked the English team of Gilbert and Sullivan to write *The Mikado*.

10. In the presidential election of 1912
   a) Woodrow Wilson won a majority of the popular vote and the Electoral College.
   b) Woodrow Wilson came in first in the popular vote, then William Howard Taft, then Theodore Roosevelt.
   c) with forty-two percent of the popular vote, Wilson had more support than any other single candidate, and won a majority in the Electoral College.
   d) the Bull Moose Party took less than six percent of the popular vote.
   e) a majority of the American electorate wanted someone other than the man who was elected president.

11. Woodrow Wilson's responses to the Mexican Revolution that began in 1910 included
   a) criticizing the military government of Victoriano Huerta, saying the United States would not deal with regimes based on irregular force rather than law.
   b) massive financial aid to the democratic government of Francisco Madero, under a proclamation calling for fourteen points to establish freedom in the country.
   c) occupying the port of Veracruz after some sailors from the United States were arrested for wandering into a section of Tampico that was off limits.
   d) endorsing a minor political party that shared Wilson's puritan Protestant morality, advocating a moral regeneration of Mexican society.
   e) sending General John J. Pershing into Mexico in pursuit of Pancho Villa, who had raided Columbus, New Mexico.

12. The assassination of President McKinley
   a) touched off a constitutional crisis over presidential succession.
   b) was almost thwarted when an African American bystander tried to deflect the bullet.
   c) provoked riots that nearly destroyed six major American cities.
   d) made war between the United States and Spain inevitable.
   e) touched off public rage against radicals, because the assassin was an anarchist.

13. Which of these were among American reactions to the war in Europe?
   a) Wilson's campaign of 1916 emphasized his efforts to distance the United States from the war.
   b) The Bull Moose Party urged entering the war in alliance with Germany.
   c) British and French seizure of neutral American ships inflamed public opinion.
   d) Republicans urged a stronger response to German violations of American rights.
   e) The public was impatient with conciliatory policies that kept the United States at peace.

## H. ESSAY QUESTIONS OR ORAL REPORTS
   1. Document the economic presence and political activity of the United Fruit Company in the nations of Central America. At its peak what fraction of the economies of these nations did the company own? What was the impact on economic and political stability, and on the standard of living for most citizens? What improvements did the company introduce? To what extent were these available to the general population? What role did United States government policy take in the company's investments and interests?

2. Examine the origin of the Federal Reserve Bank under Woodrow Wilson, and its role in subsequent years. What was its original purpose? What forces supported or opposed establishing this institution? How independent is it, or to what extent does it follow the influence of the administration holding executive power? For the last question, choose any one administration.

3. What was the scope of this nation's involvement in the Mexican Revolution from 1910 to about 1920? What positions did the federal government take? To what extent did Mexican revolutionaries find asylum or support within the United States? How did business interests in the United States position themselves? What was the long-term impact of military intervention by the United States during this period?

4. Consider what are generally grouped together as "progressive" politics from the beginning of Theodore Roosevelt's presidency to the end of Woodrow Wilson's, insofar as these politics applied to the national rather than the state governments. How did progressive politics manifest themselves in the Democratic and in the Republican party? What differing ideas did progressives hold toward concentration of power in industry, government, or other institutions? You might read Theodore Roosevelt's speech widely known under the title "New Nationalism" in defense of consolidations supervised by the government, and Woodrow Wilson's ideas collected as *The New Freedom* and looking to a less centralized economy (a position he seems in practice to have abandoned). How did the Bull Moose Party platform differ from that of the Socialist candidate Eugene V. Debs?

5. Analyze decisions of the United States Supreme Court that curtailed congressional antitrust legislation in the early years of antitrust law. What constitutional principles did the Court invoke? What alternative interpretations did the dissenting opinions offer? Offer your own conclusion about which understanding more accurately represents the meaning of the Constitution.

6. From 1898 through 1916 the United States entered one declared war and engaged in several undeclared military interventions in Latin America and one in Asia. Select one of the undeclared conflicts. Assemble facts to establish what motivated the forces the United States supported and the forces it opposed, where each drew its base of support, and what was the legal and ethical basis of the conflict. For an additional but optional task, look at tactics and strategy forced upon combatant forces by the terrain, their objectives, and the nature of their opponent.

_____

_____

_____

_____

_____

_____

_____

_____

_____

_____

_____

_____

_____

_____

_____

# Of War, Money, Preachers, and Jazz

**20**

## A. TERMS

Zimmermann telegram _____

_____

_____

neutral nations _____

_____

_____

daylight saving time _____

_____

_____

selective service _____

_____

_____

Red Scare _____

_____

_____

Volstead Act _____

_____

_____

Harlem Renaissance _____

_____

_____

multinational corporation _____

_____

_____

house-rent party _____

_____

_____

general strike _____

_____

_____

anti-Semitism _____

_____

welfare capitalism _____

_____

agricultural price supports _____

_____

## B. PHOTOGRAPHS

1. Write a brief paragraph pointing out what is false in this British propaganda poster about World War I, or write about what genuine characteristics of the German national character contributed to this view.

2. How was the steel strike organized, and by whom? Name some of the larger national or ethnic groups among the strikers.

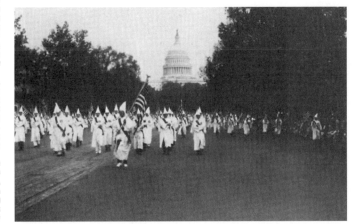

_____

_____

_____

_____

_____

_____

_____

_____

_____

_____

_____

_____

_____

_____

_____

_____

_____

_____

_____

_____

_____

_____

3. In a paragraph, explain why the Ku Klux Klan was marching openly during the mid-1920s in the nation's capital, and what political power it represented. Why did an organization claiming an ancestry in the survivors of the defeated Confederacy march behind the flag of the United States, the victor over the Confederacy?

_____

_____

_____

_____

_____

_____

_____

_____

_____

_____

_____

_____
_____
_____
_____
_____
_____
_____
_____
_____
_____
_____
_____

## C. VOCABULARY

propaganda _____
_____
_____

draft _____
_____
_____

entrenchments _____
_____
_____

mandates _____
_____
_____

anarchism _____
_____
_____

Prohibition _____
_____
_____

consumerism _____
_____
_____

lynching _____
_____
_____

Jazz Age _____
_____
_____

## D. INDIVIDUALS

Jeannette Rankin _____
_____
_____

John "Black Jack" Pershing _____
_____
_____

Carrie Catt _____
_____
_____

Woodrow Wilson _____
_____
_____

Tom Mooney _____
_____
_____

Harry Daugherty _____
_____
_____

Emma Goldman _____
_____
_____

Ole Hanson _____
_____
_____

Langston Hughes _____
_____
_____

W. E. B. Du Bois _____
_____
_____

Al Capone _____
_____
_____

Bessie Smith _____
_____
_____

A. Mitchell Palmer _____
_____
_____

Ethel Waters _____

_____

Claude McKay _____

_____

Charles Forbes _____

_____

William Simmons _____

_____

Zora Neale Hurston _____

_____

Warren G. Harding _____

_____

Marcus Garvey _____

_____

John Dos Passos _____

_____

Alice Paul _____

_____

Robert Frost _____

_____

Duke Ellington _____

_____

William Faulkner _____

_____

Henry Ford _____

_____

_____

Eugene V. Debs _____
_____
_____

Carl Sandburg _____
_____
_____

Sherwood Anderson _____
_____
_____

Sinclair Lewis _____
_____
_____

Charles Lindbergh _____
_____
_____

F. Scott Fitzgerald _____
_____
_____

## E. TRUE FALSE—circle one.

1. T F Germany had provided no warning to travelers on vessels like the *Lusitania* that its nation's U-boats might attack such ships.
2. T F Many Irish Americans opposed American support for Great Britain in its war with Germany.
3. T F International law prohibited seizure of goods, carried to enemy nations in time of war, on ships flying the flag of a neutral power.
4. T F Isolationist Republican progressives sought to keep the United States out of World War I.
5. T F After the nation's entrance into World War I, the United States officially defined itself as one of the Allies.
6. T F By 1916, almost half the western states were allowing women to vote.
7. T F The first year after the entrance of the United States into World War I, the nation's primary contribution to the war effort was in extending loans to associated European countries.
8. T F In 1919 a foreign-born anarchist accidentally blew himself up trying to plant a bomb at the front door to the home of Attorney General A. Mitchell Palmer.
9. T F German Americans welcomed the Treaty of Versailles as a return to normal relations.
10. T F The League of Nations, formed without the participation of the United States, turned out to be an effective way of preventing wars and preserving democratic government.
11. T F In 1919 the patriotic fervor that had been generated during World War I was turned against American labor unions.
12. T F General Motors differed from Ford Motor Company in allowing autonomy to managers in each division, and encouraging managers to give their subordinates a similar freedom of initiative.
13. T F In an attempt to stop Mayor Hanson's speaking tour denouncing Bolshevism, a warning letter was mailed to the Seattle mayor's office.
14. T F In the 1920s fundamentalist Protestants, who believed in the literal truth of every word in the Bible, formed close alliances with conservatives in the Roman Catholic Church.
15. T F Anti-Semitism was mainly a belief of uneducated rural people living in poverty, not of wealthy, sophisticated urban residents.

16. T F At the Scopes trial in 1925, William Jennings Bryan testified that the seven days of creation in Genesis could have been geological eras.

17. T F There was no decline in consumption of alcohol during the period of legal Prohibition in the federal Constitution.

18. T F The anti-immigrant movement of the 1920s included fundamentalist Protestants, as well as upper-class Americans who drew on a Darwinian theory of racial superiority.

19. T F In the 1920s, the Ku Klux Klan aimed at maintaining white Protestant power over blacks, Catholics, Jews, eastern and southern Europeans, and other ethnic communities.

**F. MATCHING** Draw a line connecting each work of literature at the left to its author on the right.

| | |
|---|---|
| *The Blacker the Berry* | Carl Van Vechten |
| *The Enormous Room* | John Dos Passos |
| *Home to Harlem* | Zitkala Sä |
| *Nigger Heaven* | Sinclair Lewis |
| *Three Soldiers* | Claude McKay |
| *Winesburg, Ohio* | e e cummings |
| *Main Street* | Wallace Thurman |
| *Cogewea* | Sherwood Anderson |

For each figure at the left, draw a line connecting that individual with the opponent or opposite listed at the right.

| | |
|---|---|
| George Creel | Warren G. Harding |
| Woodrow Wilson | A. Mitchell Palmer |
| Georges Clemenceau | William Jennings Bryan |
| James Cox | W. E. B. Du Bois |
| Emma Goldman | Henry Cabot Lodge |
| Clarence Darrow | Jeannette Rankin |
| Claude McKay | Calvin Coolidge |
| Robert La Follette | Kaiser Wilhelm II |

**G. FILL IN THE BLANKS.**
Fill in the missing words from Claude McKay's poem "If We Must Die" a response to the race riots of 1919.

men
cowardly
penned
fighting back
wall
inglorious
hogs

If we must die, let it not be like _____

Hunted and _____, in an _____ spot. . . .

Like _____ we'll face the murderous, _____ pack,

Pressed to the _____, dying, but _____!

**H. MULTIPLE CHOICE**—circle one or more correct answers.
1. The larger causes of the war that broke out in August 1914 include
   a) Adolf Hitler's attempt to make the German "Master Race" the rulers of Europe.
   b) a contest for naval supremacy between Britain and Germany.
   c) the defense of Christian Europe against conquest by the Muslim Ottoman Empire.
   d) competition among European powers as well as Japan for colonies.
   e) Serbia's attempt to take territory from Russia, blocked by Russia's alliance with Austria.

2. When a German U-boat torpedoed the British liner *Lusitania* in 1915,
   a) President Wilson refused to comment, and his silence led his war-minded secretary of state to resign.
   b) nearly twelve hundred people died, including 128 Americans.

c) Germany, determined to keep the United States neutral, ordered a stop to attacks on passenger liners.

d) the Congress of the United States unanimously declared war on Germany the next day.

e) British munitions on board exploded, doing more damage than the torpedo.

3. Measures adopted to suppress dissent after the United States entered World War I included
    a) the Espionage Act, allowing twenty years in prison for aiding the enemy or interfering with the draft.
    b) authorization granted to squads of special Secret Service officers to drag citizens from their homes and summarily execute them if they were suspected of antiwar sentiment.
    c) the rounding up of Americans of German descent and their removal to concentration camps.
    d) the Sedition Act, allowing imprisonment for any expression of opinion that was "disloyal, profane, scurrilous or abusive" toward the government.
    e) mob violence against Americans of German descent, though not officially encouraged by the government.

4. In the influenza epidemic toward the end of World War I,
    a) more people died from the virus than from all the battles of the war combined.
    b) for the first time a viral epidemic was stopped by a newly developed serum.
    c) the disease attacked a disproportionate number of young adults.
    d) the flu spread in a logical pattern, advancing ten miles per day in all directions.
    e) in some cities, officials required people to wear masks in public.

5. Among American immigrant communities that reacted to the Treaty of Versailles,
    a) German Americans approved of the restoration of Poland as an independent nation.
    b) Italian Americans resented the inclusion of the city of Fiume in Yugoslavia.
    c) Irish Americans welcomed the treaty for recognizing Irish independence.
    d) Arab Americans applauded mandates awarded to France and Britain in the Middle East.
    e) English immigrants demanded that the treaty punish Irish rebels for their aid to Germany during the war.

6. The Treaty of Versailles was defeated in the United States Senate because
    a) approval with amendments proposed by Senator Henry Cabot Lodge was opposed by isolationists and by Democrats loyal to President Wilson.
    b) most Americans were afraid the League of Nations would make it easier for influenza epidemics to spread around the world.
    c) Republicans wanted to squeeze a lot more money out of Germany.
    d) no version of the treaty won support from two thirds of the senators.
    e) approval of the treaty without amendments faced opposition from isolationists and supporters of Senator Lodge's amended version.

7. Seattle was convulsed by a general strike in 1919, in which
    a) Russian Bolshevik agents stirred up immigrant workers against the government.
    b) city employees, including streetcar conductors, firefighters, and secretaries, walked off their jobs in sympathy with striking longshoremen.
    c) stores, businesses, and homes of wealthy families were looted in the absence of any effective police protection.
    d) Mayor Ole Hanson invited Japanese troops to help restore order and reestablish the authority of the local, state, and federal government.
    e) strikers set up a Committee of Fifteen to insure that the public would not suffer loss of essential services.

8. The trial in 1925 of John Scopes in Dayton Tennessee for teaching evolution
    a) was presented by the defense as disproving the truth of Christianity and the Bible.
    b) was presided over by Justice Oliver Wendell Holmes.
    c) resulted in Scopes's conviction for being an atheist unfit to teach in public schools.
    d) presented a defense that Scopes had not violated Tennessee law, since his teaching of Darwin's theories did not contradict Scripture.
    e) made William Jennings Bryan a national hero, who in later years was acclaimed as a Democratic candidate for president.

9. Anti-immigrant movements in the 1920s exalted Protestants of northern European descent over
    a) immigrants from eastern and southern Europe, thought of as strange and inferior.
    b) Irish Catholics, even though they had been in the United States for generations.
    c) Mormons and *braceros* who had driven white settlers out of the Southwest.
    d) French Canadians, suspected of smuggling firearms to western Indian tribes.
    e) refugees from British, French, and German colonies in Africa.

10. The Ku Klux Klan revival, beginning in 1915 at Stone Mountain, Georgia,
    a) drew most of its membership from Mississippi, Alabama, Louisiana, and Texas.
    b) tried to hold a parade in Washington, D.C., but was never able to do so.
    c) preached passionate patriotism to the United States rather than a sentimental loyalty to the Civil War Confederacy.
    d) centered in rural areas, for city residents were too sophisticated to join.
    e) reached at its height a membership of over four million.

11. Harlem became remarkable and widely known in the period after World War I for
    a) being one urban area where African Americans owned most of the real estate.
    b) benefiting from a remarkably extensive program by the city government promoting black migration to the community.
    c) having an assertive social and cultural self-identity.
    d) offering to black migrants from the rural South the tempo of a cosmopolitan northern city.
    e) being wracked by frequent riots that made it impossible for whites to patronize the area's night clubs.

12. The innovations introduced by Henry Ford's enterprise included
    a) the earliest automobiles.
    b) an eight-hour day paying workers $5 an hour.
    c) a Sociological Department that looked into home conditions of employees.
    d) tolerance of employees who drank.
    e) an assembly line that moved continuously rather than by a succession of starts and stops.

13. The Nineteenth Amendment, guaranteeing women the vote, came
    a) many years after several states granted women the vote, western states having viewed them as carriers of peaceful domestic values badly needed in newly settled areas.
    b) when millions of women refused to share the bed with their husbands until the amendment was ratified.
    c) at a time when numbers of women were entering the social work and health professions, and a peace movement led by women such as Jane Addams was fresh in the public memory.
    d) after Congress and state legislatures decided it would not make much difference anyway, since most women would vote the way their husbands told them to vote.
    e) after a war in which suffragists who cooperated with the war effort argued that providing women the vote would contribute to national unity.

14. At one time or another in American history the agitation for reform of drinking habits, which culminated in Prohibition, came from
    a) bootleggers who saw an expanded national market if the federal government banned alcohol.

b) chemical engineers who wanted to keep the supply of alcohol for use in scientific laboratory experiments.

c) Americans of property and social standing who immersed themselves in reform causes.

d) religious revivals calling on converts to lead lives of sobriety, piety, and hard work.

e) nativists who associated drinking and taverns with immigration.

15. Between the Armistice ending World War I and the coming of the Depression, economic conditions included

a) massive unemployment from 1920 to 1922.

b) mechanization of agriculture, including the use of cheap tractors running on gasoline.

c) a sharp rise in real wages for most Americans.

d) a pool of low-paid workers made up of black and white migrants from the South.

e) the coming of electricity to most American homes by 1928.

## I. ESSAY QUESTIONS OR ORAL REPORTS

1. Provide a more detailed account of how the mobilization effort for World War I appeared to fulfill many Progressive dreams of bringing closer cooperation between government and business, drawing on advances in technical knowledge, increases in social planning, and organization of public opinion. Did the results fulfill Progressive expectations?

2. Analyze the adoption of the Sixteenth, Seventeenth, Eighteenth, and Nineteenth amendments to the Constitution during the later Progressive Era. For each amendment, summarize the efforts in the previous half-century or so in favor of the principle underlying it. Why did so many fundamental changes receive approval during this period? What place did war preparedness have in the ratification of the Eighteenth Amendment and the Nineteenth? What did each of the four amendments contribute to the life of the nation?

3. Present an argument for or against the legality of the Palmer raids launched by Wilson's attorney general A. Mitchell Palmer. Cite sources originating at the time and your own reading of the Constitution. Look up what Louis Post, a government official at the time who resisted the raids, had to say about them in testimony before a committee of the House of Representatives and in his own writings. Compare Palmer's decisions, and the raids, with actions of the federal government during other periods of political tension in the United States, such as the Civil War, the Cold War, and the period after September 11, 2001.

4. Study and document the impact of the automobile on American life between 1905 and 1929. Include the number of cars produced each year, the social and economic classes that used them, and changes the automobile may have made in urban growth, related industries, employment patterns, criminal enterprise, and social conditions.

5. Analyze Robert M. La Follette's Progressive Party candidacy for president in 1924. How did previous political trends contribute to this campaign? What did La Follette's platform offer that the Republican and Democratic platforms did not? Where did his support come from, regionally, occupationally, economically, socially, and ethnically, and why did he draw these groups and not others?

6. Argue for or against J. Walter Thompson's pronouncement that the typical American had the intelligence of a fourteen year old. How has the development of advertising in the past eighty years refuted or sustained Thompson's view? If it was accurate then, is it still accurate today, or are American consumers more mature and sophisticated? This question requires a degree of speculation and judgment on your part, but be sure not to lapse into opinion unsupported by some evidence.

7. Develop your own answer to the argument between W. E. B. Du Bois and writers in the tradition of Claude McKay over portrayal of African American life in literature. Extend your conclusions to later forms of entertainment, such as movies and mass-produced musical records, tapes, and CD's.

# Hitting Bottom and Climbing Back Up

## 21

## A. TERMS

Dust Bowl _____
_____
_____

New Deal _____
_____
_____

sit-down strike _____
_____
_____

stock market _____
_____
_____

migrant worker _____
_____
_____

tribal governments _____
_____
_____

Bonus Army _____
_____
_____

class warfare _____
_____
_____

collective bargaining _____
_____
_____

public works _____
_____
_____

## B. PHOTOGRAPHS

1. Explain what causes the price of stock to rise. How is this process related to real processes of production and exchange, and how are the two distinct? Why are there bubbles of rising stock prices, followed by a puncture of the bubble?

2. Pick any two photos taken by Dorothea Lange and reproduced on pages 636, 655–662, or 670. For each, write half a page indicating as best you can what the focal figure in the photo must have been thinking about the situation at the time and what the future might be.

_____

_____

_____

_____

_____

_____

_____

_____

_____

_____

_____

_____

_____

_____

_____

_____

_____

_____

_____

_____

_____

_____

_____

_____

_____

_____

_____

_____

_____

_____

_____

_____

_____

_____

3. Why, in your estimation, would labor troubles bring on clashes with police, or include tactics as confrontational as sit-down strikes?

_____

_____

_____

_____

_____

_____

_____

_____

_____

_____

_____

_____

_____

_____

_____

_____

_____

_____

_____

_____

_____

_____

_____

_____

## C. VOCABULARY

Okies _____

_____

confidence _____

_____

stock puts _____

_____

rumrunners _____

_____

hobo _____

_____

vigilantes _____

_____

tycoons _____

_____

pension _____

_____

foreclosure _____

_____

## D. INDIVIDUALS

Franklin D. Roosevelt _____

_____

Walter Reuther _____

_____

Douglas MacArthur _____

_____

_____

Huey Pierce Long _____

_____

_____

Herbert Hoover _____

_____

_____

John Steinbeck _____

_____

_____

Hugh S. Johnson _____

_____

_____

Dorothea Lange _____

_____

_____

Frances Perkins _____

_____

_____

John Llewellyn Lewis _____

_____

_____

Milo Reno _____

_____

_____

Norman Thomas _____

_____

_____

Charles Coughlin _____

_____

_____

Harry Hopkins _____

_____

_____

Francis Townsend _____

_____

_____

Upton Sinclair _____

_____

_____

## E. ORGANIZATIONS

Unemployed Councils _____
_____
_____

Farm Holiday movement _____
_____
_____

Southern Tenant Farmers Union _____
_____
_____

Congress of Industrial Organizations _____
_____
_____

United Mine Workers _____
_____
_____

Share Croppers Union _____
_____
_____

United Automobile Workers _____
_____
_____

American Liberty League _____
_____
_____

United Rubber Workers _____
_____
_____

International Brotherhood of Teamsters _____
_____
_____

American Federation of Labor _____
_____
_____

Communist Party _____
_____
_____

American Legion _____
_____
_____

Cannery and Agricultural Workers Industrial Union _____

_____

Citizens Alliance _____

_____

_____

Socialist Party _____

_____

_____

## F. TRUE FALSE—circle one.

1. T F  In the mid-1930s, when coal trains slowed down in towns, local residents would hop on and off the cars stealing pieces of coal to heat their homes.

2. T F  Coal miners and southern textile workers were among the first to benefit from the booming economy of the later 1920s.

3. T F  When stock prices collapsed on Tuesday, October 29, 1929, billions of dollars in invested funds evaporated.

4. T F  The Reconstruction Finance Corporation of 1932 provided a few public works projects, but its main intention was to rescue large banks so better times would trickle down to the public in general.

5. T F  To verify that a family was poor enough to qualify for free food, officials would measure the thickness of the leather on the soles of a child's shoes.

6. T F  President Franklin D. Roosevelt began the first program to buy agricultural crops in bad times and hold them off the market until prices rose.

7. T F  Although times were hard in the Depression, unemployed providers were not reduced to acts of petty theft.

8. T F  General Douglas MacArthur commanded federal troops who attacked World War I veterans from the Bonus Army encamped in the District of Columbia in 1932.

9. T F  When two truck drivers were killed and sixty-seven wounded in Minneapolis in 1934, the Citizens Alliance urged calm and restored a sense of reasoned compromise to the city.

10. T F  In Akron, Ohio, in 1936 police deputized men to clear the Goodyear factory of striking rubber workers; workers from all over the city came to confront them.

11. T F  Acts of industrial insurgency in 1935 demonstrated that workers could shut down an entire assembly line by causing a snag at one point in its operation.

12. T F  Protection offered by the National Industrial Recovery Act allowed rapid unionization of farm laborers in California by 1937, quickly curbing police and vigilante violence.

13. T F  American Legion posts in California organized protection for striking farm workers from police and private grower security forces.

14. T F  The American Liberty League was organized for the purpose of building support for the New Deal among businessmen.

15. T F  Father Charles Coughlin blamed the Depression on Communists, Jews, and Wall Street while promoting programs to help the poor.

16. T F  In 1936, Franklin Roosevelt was reelected with nearly sixty-one percent of the popular vote, losing only the states of Vermont and Maine.

17. T F  At the start of the twentieth century, three-fourths of the American people lived on farms; by 1930 only one in ten people did so.

18. T F  By 1933 many farms were being foreclosed because farmers could not obtain enough income to pay off loans secured by their land.

19. T F  A medical examiner called in to investigate the accusation of rape in the Scottsboro case testified that physical evidence did not support the charge, and an alleged victim of rape withdrew her claim.

20. T F  Hiring by the Tennessee Valley Authority favored black over white workers.

94

21.  T  F  After the Daughters of the American Revolution refused to let Eleanor Roosevelt speak in Constitution Hall, Marian Anderson resigned from the organization.

22.  T  F  In Tucson, Arizona, officials in charge of relief during the Depression distributed money on a scale that differentiated between white, Indian, Hispanic American, and refugee Mexican recipients.

**G. MATCHING** Draw a line connecting the New Deal agency at left with the appropriate description on the right.

| | |
|---|---|
| Civilian Conservation Corps | built bridges and highways |
| Federal Emergency Relief Administration | cut the supply of farm produce in order to raise the price farmers received for their goods |
| Civil Works Administration | provided work for young men set to rescuing and preserving depleted natural resources |
| Public Works Administration | hired artists to paint murals on public buildings or engage in creative literature |
| Federal Housing Administration | furnished money to local governments for building schools, playgrounds, bridges, libraries, and sewers |
| Agricultural Adjustment Administration | distributed relief funds to states |
| Works Progress Administration | supplied loans to middle-income families for home construction and repair and for mortgage payments |

# H. FILL IN THE BLANKS.

One of President Roosevelt's most famous quotations:

"The only thing we have to _____ is _____ itself— nameless, unreasoning, unjustified _____."

The "Blue Eagle" was the symbol of the _____.

A North Carolina mill worker remarked that "Mr. _____ is the only man we ever had in the _____ who would understand that my _____ is a _____."

The slogan for Huey P. Long's "_____ Our Wealth" program was "Every man a _____, but no one wears a _____."

John L. Lewis of the United Mine Workers spread the claim that "The _____ wants you to join a _____."

crown
terror
President
White House
Share
boss
sonofabitch
fear
king
National Recovery Administration
union
Roosevelt
fear

# I. MULTIPLE CHOICE—circle one or more correct answers.

1. During the economic troubles known as the Great Depression,
   a) a great number of banks closed their doors in 1931 and 1932 because of defaulted loans.
   b) in November 1929 nearly ten million American workers were laid off.
   c) by 1933 gross production nationwide had shrunk by half.
   d) rampant looting and gang wars nearly tore New York City apart in 1930.
   e) Treasury Secretary Andrew Mellon resigned in protest against President Hoover's slowness in meeting the emergency.

2. During the Depression, Americans who drifted across the continent
   a) found work in regions with growing industry, relieving states where new jobs were not being created and unemployment had increased.
   b) joined the ranks of hoboes and migrant workers.
   c) switched from manual labor to the growing numbers of office workers.
   d) included large numbers of adolescents of both genders, traveling in packs.
   e) sometimes found odd jobs to earn a meal, sometimes begged at back doors for handouts, sometimes were treated harshly by police.

3. Among the means unemployed Americans turned to for survival in the Depression were
   a) the invention of industries such as computer technology that created their own markets.
   b) the sale of fruits and vegetables from pushcarts.
   c) the cultivation of coca leaf to sell to the Coca-Cola company.
   d) the sale of brushes, cosmetics, Bibles, and encyclopedias door to door.
   e) the sale of junk and scrap metal.

4. The bank holiday declared by President Roosevelt in 1933 meant that
   a) employees of banks got five days of paid vacation every year in addition to Christmas.
   b) private ownership of banks was outlawed; all were taken over by the government.
   c) banks were closed for five days to stop a run of panic withdrawals.
   d) every bank was examined by the treasury department before reopening.
   e) banks were required to close at 3:00 pm every weekday and all day Saturday.

5. In decisions that went against the New Deal, the Supreme Court
   a) declared the Agricultural Adjustment Administration an unconstitutional exercise of the federal power to regulate interstate commerce.
   b) overturned the National Labor Relations Act as an unconstitutional infringement on the property rights of employers.
   c) prohibited the Army Corps of Engineers from building dams unless the site was on a river that defined an interstate boundary.
   d) ruled that Franklin D. Roosevelt could not run for a third presidential term.
   e) found the National Industrial Recovery Act an unconstitutional delegation to the executive branch of powers reserved to Congress.

6. Which of these statements would describe the lives of coal miners in Harlan County, Kentucky, in 1932?
   a) Mine owners provided a comprehensive system of medical care and free housing.
   b) Miners had to buy from company stores, were fired for shopping elsewhere, and in many cases were paid in script accepted only by the company store.
   c) Miners without union protection were marched into the mines in chain gangs, watched by overseers armed with machine guns.
   d) Company towns were built with little concern for sanitation, and rent for miners' shacks was deducted from their paychecks by the company.
   e) The Depression closed down mines and made the lives of miners even worse.

7. The most important sit-down strikes of the 1930s included
   a) the nationwide occupation of McDonnell-Douglass plants by the International Association of Machinists and Aerospace Workers in 1939.
   b) protests at the Firestone plant in Akron, Ohio, in 1936.
   c) a strike, led by Communists, of federal employees who in 1938 occupied the Office of Price Administration in the wake of the Molotov-Ribbentrop pact.
   d) sit-down strikes in the onion fields of McAllen, Texas, and the cotton fields of Tulare, California, in 1934, organized by John Steinbeck and Upton Sinclair.
   e) a strike in late 1937 by the United Auto Workers at the General Motors Fisher Body Plants 1 and 2 in Flint, Michigan.

8. The Southern Tenant Farmers Union
   a) engaged in 1934 in a series of founding meetings in Tyronza, Arkansas.
   b) had a white president, a black vice president, and an interracial membership.
   c) received funding from the National Recovery Act to open offices in 157 counties.
   d) engaged in a strike during the cotton-picking season of 1935 that won wage concessions.
   e) won acceptance by large landowners eager for a stable, prosperous workforce.

9. The Fair Labor Standards Act of 1938 provided
   a) protection against discrimination based on race, color, gender, or religion.
   b) federal standards for minimum wages and maximum hours of work.
   c) detailed limitations on federal injunctions against labor unions.
   d) free universal medical care.
   e) prohibition of the use of child labor in products sold in interstate commerce.

10. Among the less successful exercises of power in Roosevelt's second term were
   a) a scheme to pack the Supreme Court with justices favorable to his programs.
   b) a vigorous effort to secure congressional approval of an anti-lynching law.
   c) plans to nationalize ownership of the steel, rail, textile, and munitions industries.
   d) sponsorship of exiles trying to overthrow the Somoza government in Nicaragua.
   e) an attempt to purge the Democratic Party of congressional candidates insufficiently supportive of his policies.

11. In response to farm foreclosures and evictions,
   a) crowds of neighbors made bids of a few cents per item, returning them to the impoverished owner.
   b) communities wrote to radio game shows to secure a chance for destitute families to play.
   c) armed neighbors in one instance trained guns on sheriff deputies to prevent foreclosure sales.
   d) communities wrote proposals to the Rockefeller Foundation for a fund to pay off mortgages.
   e) judges who ordered foreclosures were harassed.

12. The Supreme Court's reasons for throwing out convictions of the Scottsboro Boys were that
   a) the evidence clearly showed that all the defendants were innocent.
   b) no person of African descent could get a fair trial in Alabama, and so all convictions of black defendants in the state must be voided.
   c) the defendants had not had time to prepare an adequate defense.
   d) no evidence showed what state the train had been in when the crime was committed.
   e) African Americans had been systematically excluded from the jury pool.

13. Federal development of the Tennessee River Valley was
   a) advanced by the Communist Party through members working for the government.
   b) first advocated in the 1920s by Republican Senator George Norris of Nebraska.
   c) the source of clean, non-polluting electric power for eighty percent of rural Appalachia.
   d) begun in 1933 by the Tennessee Valley Authority.
   e) intended to control floods and generate power through a series of dams.

14. During the Depression, the poorest agricultural workers in the United States
    a) received adequate income from their share of agricultural adjustment payments.
    b) were forced off the land in large numbers by reduction in agricultural production.
    c) endured violent reprisals when they attempted to organize themselves.
    d) obtained great tracts of land purchased by the government, which encouraged them to develop cooperative farms.
    e) were aided by the Communists and Socialists in their efforts to organize.

15. The main differences between the AFL and the CIO during the 1930s were that
    a) the AFL was controlled by Communists while the CIO was led by John L. Lewis.
    b) the CIO organized all workers in an industry, from the most skilled to the least skilled; the AFL concentrated on the skilled and more highly paid craft workers.
    c) it was the CIO unions that were more closely associated with the large confrontational sit-down strikes that gave the labor movement of the era much of its flair.
    d) like the UMWA, the CIO refused to admit African Americans as members, while the AFL welcomed workers of all races.
    e) workers distrusted the AFL because it had a history of flirting with utopian socialist experiments rather than concentrating on wages and benefits.

## J. ESSAY QUESTIONS OR ORAL REPORTS

1. Examine the funding mechanism adopted for Social Security, and alternatives proposed at the time the program was debated and then passed into law. Of Roosevelt's plan to put into their fund a portion of an employee's wages, Senator Huey P. Long of Louisiana observed that a "poor wage earner will be allowed to help his aged father or mother and take away a little more from his wife and children." How has experience since 1935 demonstrated the wisdom or weakness of supporting Social Security by a payroll tax?

2. Develop an overview of one or more major labor battles of the 1930s. This could take the form of assembling detailed facts about one strike. Or it could be a more general study of the entire period, a comparison of two or more different struggles, or a concentration on a category, such as the CIO, the AFL, general strikes, agriculture, textile organizing in the Southeast, or the role of the Socialist or Communist Party.

3. Pick one or more New Deal programs and present an analysis of what were the original stated purposes, how well these purposes were met, and what if any were the unanticipated effects on American life.

4. Trace the causes of the dust storms that ravaged the Great Plains during the 1930s, from the first attempts to farm the region up to the agricultural techniques in use during the early twentieth century. Could alternative patterns of settlement and agriculture have avoided the conditions that produced the dust storms? Was there in those days any information or any kind of thinking about the environment that might have forewarned the farmers about the disaster that would afflict later inhabitants of the region?

5. Detail the changes in federal government policy toward American Indians during the Depression. Draw your own conclusion as to whether the changes were an improvement, and what might have been done better.

6. Imagine on your own a publicity campaign for Upton Sinclair's EPIC or Senator Huey P. Long's Share Our Wealth. Analyze what demographic constituencies such a campaign might expect to win over and what groups of voters would be firmly opposed, and consider how arguments might be framed that would appeal to sections of the population likely to be drawn to the program.

# World War II and Its Prelude  22

## A. TERMS

Vichy France _____
_____
_____

gold standard _____
_____
_____

Good Neighbor Policy _____
_____
_____

war profiteering _____
_____
_____

neutrality acts _____
_____
_____

cash and carry _____
_____
_____

fascism _____
_____
_____

Bushido _____
_____
_____

Aryan _____
_____
_____

Popular Front _____
_____
_____

*Blitzkrieg* _____

_____

_____

lend-lease _____

_____

_____

Four Freedoms _____

_____

_____

trench foot _____

_____

_____

Bataan Death March _____

_____

_____

## B. PHOTOGRAPHS

Why was this kind of conservation important to the national war effort? How did the munitions industry change in later years, so that similar appeals were not made during the Vietnam War or the Persian Gulf War, or in support of troops dispatched to Afghanistan or Iraq?

Save waste fats for explosives

TAKE THEM TO YOUR MEAT DEALER

## C. VOCABULARY

isolationism _____
_____
_____

belligerent _____
_____
_____

fasces _____
_____
_____

*bracero* _____
_____
_____

*pachuco* _____
_____
_____

hedgerow _____
_____
_____

*issei* _____
_____
_____

*nisei* _____
_____
_____

kamikaze _____
_____
_____

cryptography _____
_____
_____

## D. INDIVIDUALS

Gerald P. Nye _____
_____
_____

Joseph W. "Vinegar Joe" Stilwell _____
_____
_____

Augusto Cesar Sandino _____

_____

Benito Mussolini _____

_____

Anastasio Somoza _____

_____

Adolf Hitler _____

_____

Winston Churchill _____

_____

George C. Marshall _____

_____

Mao Zedong _____

_____

A. Philip Randolph _____

_____

Herbert Hoover _____

_____

Neville Chamberlain _____

_____

Gerd von Rundstedt _____

_____

Francisco Franco _____

_____

Edward R. Murrow _____

_____

NAME _____  DATE _____

Franklin Delano Roosevelt (as commander-in-chief) _____
_____
_____

Jonathan Wainwright _____
_____
_____

Anthony C. McAuliffe _____
_____
_____

Wendell Wilkie _____
_____
_____

Chester Nimitz _____
_____
_____

George C. Patton _____
_____
_____

Joseph Stalin _____
_____
_____

Philippe Pétain _____
_____
_____

Erwin Rommel _____
_____
_____

Chiang Kai-shek _____
_____
_____

Charles de Gaulle _____
_____
_____

## E. ORGANIZATIONS AND PROJECTS
League of Nations _____
_____
_____

London Naval Conference _____
_____
_____

National Socialist German Labor Party _____
_____
_____

Office of Price Administration _____
_____
_____

National War Labor Board _____
_____
_____

United Service Organization _____
_____
_____

Brotherhood of Sleeping Car Porters _____
_____
_____

Manhattan Project _____
_____
_____

## F. TRUE FALSE—circle one.

1. T  F  Early in World War II United States military services were concerned that French islands in the Caribbean could be used as bases to attack the American coastline.
2. T  F  An undeclared war engaged United States ships and the German navy months before Pearl Harbor, as the United States tried to protect British shipping in the Atlantic.
3. T  F  Teams of Nazi saboteurs, slipped into several points on the east coast of the United States, wreaked considerable damage on war industries and cities in 1942.
4. T  F  When the Mexican government nationalized oil lands owned by citizens of the United States, FDR sent marines to seize several Mexican cities.
5. T  F  For some time after the United States entered World War II, the cities on the east coast remained brightly lighted clearly defining the outlines of ships at night, which made them easy targets for U-boats.
6. T  F  The United States made special provisions in the immigration laws to accept thousands of German Jewish refugees between 1935 and 1939.
7. T  F  During World War II, the merchant marine would have been attractive to radicals who scorned military discipline, but wanted to fight a workers' war against fascism.
8. T  F  The Somoza family, put in power by American military intervention in 1926, ruled Nicaragua for decades, looting the country's wealth through massive corruption.
9. T  F  When Nazi Germany invaded Poland in 1939, the Soviet Union came to the defense of the Poles, and war between Germany and the USSR began immediately.
10. T  F  French Field Marshal Philippe Pétain, a hero of World War I, carried on from his headquarters in Vichy a heroic resistance to the Nazi occupation.
11. T  F  Japanese military strategy was based on the theory that Japan could win a long war of attrition with the United States, which would run out of industrial capacity.
12. T  F  The Japanese attack at Pearl Harbor on December 7, 1941, destroyed part of the American fleet but found no aircraft carriers in the harbor.

13. T F After months of fighting, Japanese forces forced the surrender in the Philippines of a combined Filipino and American army of 80,000.

14. T F President Roosevelt forcefully reminded General MacArthur early in the war that the president is the commander-in-chief of the armed forces, and MacArthur was humbled.

15. T F After the first year of United States participation in World War II, American industry supplied ships, tanks, and aircraft in numbers that no other nation on earth could match.

16. T F The pain and suffering inflicted on civilians in the United States during World War II exceeded that experienced in all of Europe and Asia combined.

17. T F In one of the worst race riots in the history of Los Angeles, Mexican American zoot suiters ran through the city beating up white servicemen, as police watched helplessly.

18. T F General industrial preparedness and production of war orders for Britain ended the Depression.

19. T F Throughout American engagement in World War II, African American soldiers were assigned to racially segregated units, serving primarily under white officers.

20. T F Military service in World War II provided some ethnic reconciliation among Americans of different backgrounds who were thrown together and fought side by side.

21. T F Most of the fighting against Germany was done by the United States, supported by Great Britain, while the Soviet Union fought off a few German divisions in the east.

22. T F President Roosevelt announced in 1943 that if the Axis powers agreed to surrender, the Allies would grant them "reasonable and honorable terms" to get the war over.

23. T F In 1943 Mussolini was dismissed from the Italian government; the new government switched sides to the Allies while German troops continued to occupy parts of Italy.

24. T F Allied troops moving in fixed lines of battle confounded German motorized units in Normandy and slowly pressed the enemy back on a broad front.

25. T F American ingenuity overcame a constantly threatened shortage of supplies and ammunition, which the Germans were able to produce in greater abundance.

26. T F Japanese soldiers in World War II refused to surrender, because it was dishonorable and because they expected to be tortured, but once made prisoner, astonished soldiers guarding them by their obedience, no longer servants of the Emperor of Japan.

27. T F The struggle for Okinawa from April to June 1945 took the lives of seventy thousand Japanese soldiers, over seventy-six hundred Americans on land, nearly five thousand sailors killed by kamikaze attacks, and more than a hundred thousand Okinawan civilians.

28. T F Although some military leaders wanted to leapfrog past the Philippines to reach Japan, General MacArthur retook the islands quickly with minimal casualties.

## G. FILL THE BLANKS.

1. Gearing up for war production, President Roosevelt observed that "In some communities _____ dislike to hire women. In others they are reluctant to hire _____. We can no longer _____ to indulge such prejudices."

2. Fanny Christina Hill's sister observed that for many African Americans "_____ was the one that got us _____ of the _____."

3. Two important turning points in World War II were the battle of aircraft carriers at _____ and the German surrender at _____.

terror
hedgerows
Hitler
white folks' kitchen
Chinese
out
civilian
tanks
Midway
employers
invent
supplies
Himalayan
service stations
Negroes
military reserves
Stalingrad
afford

107

4. The Flying Tigers flew _____ to the _____
over the _____ Mountains.

5. American aerial bombing strategy during World War II emphasized hitting _____.
British air strikes were intended to inflict

_____ on _____ populations, a policy the Americans
came to only later in the conflict.

6. In Normandy, Allied troops were surprised by _____ dividing up the land.
American soldiers had to _____ new tools. Young men who had worked in

_____ put damaged _____ back together.

## H. MULTIPLE CHOICE—circle one or more correct answers.
1. Which of these statements correctly describe the naval war for control of the North Atlantic in 1942?
   a) Wealthy yachtsmen drove U-boats from the Atlantic by reporting their position when they surfaced for air.
   b) For a time German submarines conducted a damaging campaign against merchant ships near the North American coastline.
   c) The disastrous convoy system concentrated large numbers of ships that became easy targets for U-boats.
   d) German submarines communicated by codes so complex that Allied cryptographers were never able to break them.
   e) Aircraft that could pick off submarines when they surfaced made a decisive difference, both near the coast and farther out in the Atlantic.

2. The Kellogg-Briand Pact, negotiated during Calvin Coolidge's presidential term, was
   a) a treaty that made possible the resistance to Adolf Hitler's program of conquest in Europe.
   b) an example of American imperialism, forcing impoverished nations to purchase large quantities of surplus breakfast cereal.
   c) an attempt to outlaw war.
   d) the product of allowing a few Wilsonian Democrats to sneak into the cabinet during three Republican administrations.
   e) an ineffectual exercise in good will signed by over sixty military powers.

3. The character of the League of Nations in the 1930s can be measured by
   a) the expulsion of invading Italian armies from Ethiopia by an international force.
   b) its success in negotiating the withdrawal of Japanese forces from Manchuria.
   c) the refusal by member nations to enforce economic sanctions against Italy.
   d) the prompt coordinated international response to the Rape of Nanking.
   e) the development of a comprehensive plan for independence of African colonies.

4. Nazi measures against German Jews, prior to World War II, included
   a) the Nuremberg Laws, limiting Jewish civil rights and employment.
   b) the removal of urban Jews to rural agricultural cooperatives separate from Aryans.
   c) the deportation of Jews to Palestine to establish a Jewish homeland outside of Germany.
   d) *Kristallnacht*, when gangs attacked Jewish shops and other buildings.
   e) the removal of German Jews to concentration camps.

5. When General Francisco Franco led a rebellion against the elected government of Spain,
   a) Britain, France, and the United States pledged to support Spanish democracy.
   b) conservatives, fascists, and the Roman Catholic hierarchy supported Franco.
   c) the Soviet Union and Nazi Germany reached an agreement to partition Spain.

    d) American volunteers fought for the elected republican government of Spain.

    e) Germany and Italy supported Franco with massive aerial bombing.

6. Events that preceded the outbreak of World War II included
    a) Austria's rejection of all Hitler's attempts to unite the two nations.
    b) a treaty signed at Munich that turned over the Sudetenland of Czechoslovakia to Hitler.
    c) Hitler's gobbling up of the rest of Czechoslovakia, violating his promises at Munich.
    d) a mutual defense pact between Poland and the Soviet Union.
    e) Neville Chamberlain's guarantee that his government would support the independence of Poland in the face of threats by Hitler.

7. During initial fighting by British and French forces against Germany in 1940,
    a) mobile German units went around France's fortified Maginot line on their way to an invasion of northern France.
    b) about 338,000 British and French troops were evacuated from the northern French port of Dunkirk to escape capture by the German army.
    c) Holland, Belgium, and Luxemburg betrayed France by secretly signing an alliance with Germany.
    d) France offered to settle border questions with Germany in exchange for an end to the German invasion.
    e) Winston Churchill offered independence to all British colonial possessions whose peoples contributed troops to the defense of Britain.

8. Within a few weeks of the attack on Pearl Harbor, Japan captured
    a) Sydney and Melbourne in Australia.
    b) Hong Kong and Singapore from the British.
    c) many of the Hawaiian islands.
    d) Easter Island, Tierra del Fuego, and Pitcairn Island.
    e) the Dutch East Indies (most of which is now Indonesia).

9. The relocation of Japanese Americans to internment camps often away from the West Coast
    a) was a voluntary option many families sought for their own protection.
    b) resulted in massive loss of family property by theft or quick sale.
    c) interrupted the respect that whites in western states had traditionally demonstrated toward Asians.
    d) did not lessen the effectiveness of a combat unit of Japanese Americans.
    e) received approval from the Supreme Court on the grounds of "real military dangers."

10. In the Battle of Guadalcanal, fought just after the American naval victory at Midway,
    a) marines swarmed over the unprepared Japanese defenders in two weeks.
    b) American soldiers enjoyed a well-stocked Post Exchange, while Japanese troops suffered in miserable jungle encampments.
    c) the first naval attempt to resupply the American force on the island failed.
    d) American supplies ran low, and Japanese supplies even lower.
    e) both sides endured misery beyond the normal horrors of war until American forces obtained control of the island early in 1943.

11. What perspective did Allied leaders bring to the debate whether to send a force across the Channel from Britain to invade France, then under German occupation, in addition to pursuing the Mediterranean campaign?
    a) Stalin wanted the Red Army to go all the way to Paris, and did not wish for British and other troops from the West to get there before him.
    b) Churchill wanted to concentrate on insuring the success of the Western Allies in the Mediterranean, a body of water vital to maintaining the British Empire, and to get Western troops into southeastern Europe ahead of the Red Army.

c) American military leaders, especially the army's chief of staff General George C. Marshall, thought the Mediterrranean campaign slow and cumbersome.

d) The Soviet Union was fighting the largest number of German divisions, and wanted an invasion of France to take pressure off the eastern front.

e) General De Gaulle sought the speedy liberation of France, which President Roosevelt felt obligated to honor in memory of the Marquis de Lafayette.

12. The D-Day landing on the beaches of Normandy was meticulously planned, but
    a) German forces had advance notice and were well prepared to meet it.
    b) weather, sea, and general confusion of battle left waves of individual soldiers fighting their way forward with little discipline or purpose.
    c) sheer weight of numbers is what pushed German defenders back the first day.
    d) most soldiers in the first waves of troops from the United States had never seen combat before.
    e) at the last moment Winston Churchill withdrew British support for the operation.

13. Naval forces fighting for control of islands in the Pacific held by the Japanese
    a) were often diverted to provide air cover for Chiang Kai-shek's forces driving back Japanese occupation armies in China.
    b) had fewer troops than the Japanese, but could generally assemble enough forces around any one island to overwhelm the defenders.
    c) were delayed fighting for Tarawa until the end of 1944.
    d) incapacitated most of the Japanese navy's air war ability in the first half of 1944.
    e) had occasional firefights with competing Russian naval forces in 1943.

14. Factors that determined the timing of the Japanese surrender at the end of World War II included
    a) the dropping of an atomic bomb on Hiroshima.
    b) the Japanese government's effort to hold out for a conditional surrender.
    c) the dropping of a second atomic bomb, this time on Nagasaki.
    d) Emperor Hirohito's public acceptance of unconditional surrender.
    e) the submission by the entire Japanese officer corps to Hirohito's action, for despite the hostility of the officers to the surrender, honor bound them to obey their emperor.

15. Fighting by American forces in western Europe in the last year of the war included
    a) a race to get to Berlin before the Red Army.
    b) finding a bridge across the Rhine River into the heart of Germany.
    c) making contact with German officers prepared to overthrow Hitler.
    d) breaking through the Siegfried Line west of the Rhine River.
    e) breaking a German counterattack in the Battle of the Bulge.

## I. ESSAY QUESTIONS OR ORAL REPORTS

1. Consider the formation of the Axis alliance, or as it was known at the beginning, the Anti-Comintern Alliance. In what ways did the motives of the German government differ from those of the Italians? What did they find in common in their political philosophies? How did the philosophy of the Japanese differ from the ideologies of their European partners?

2. Explain the reasons why the later Western Allies of Britain, France, and the United States failed to confront the German and Italian intervention in favor of Franco in Spain, and did not stand up to Hitler in his successful effort to grab Czechoslovakia. The topic will require you to consider both the military conditions of the time and what each of the three non-fascist Western nations was after in foreign policy.

3. Analyze any major battle of World War II, including the evacuation from Dunkirk, or any theater of significant guerrilla activity. Choose one or more perspectives from which to study the battle or theater of operations: strategic position, tactics, logistics, use of terrain, involve-

ment of civilians or effect on them, political motivations, or impact on the ultimate course of the war.

4. What shaped American policy, and that of the British, during the 1930s toward the situation in China? One good source to begin with is *Stilwell and the American Experience in China* by Barbara Tuchman.

5. Assemble data from original documents, memoirs, and other primary sources concerning the moral and military questions American leaders asked of themselves as they considered whether to drop an atomic bomb on Japan.

6. Trace the development of American public opinion from firm opposition to involvement in another European war, through the national unity supporting the war effort from 1941 to 1945. Identify the different strands of isolationist political philosophy. Discover whether any of them changed once war approached or broke out, and if they changed, how they explained the continuity or distinction between their two positions. A good source on one famous American's isolationism is Randy Roberts and David Welky, *Charles A. Lindbergh: The Power and Peril of Celebrity* (Brandywine, 2003).

_____
_____
_____
_____
_____
_____
_____
_____
_____
_____
_____
_____
_____
_____
_____
_____
_____
_____
_____
_____
_____
_____
_____
_____
_____
_____
_____
_____
_____

# Warm Hearths and a Cold War

## 23

## A. TERMS

Truman Doctrine _____
_____
_____

iron curtain _____
_____
_____

Marshall Plan _____
_____
_____

Cold War _____
_____
_____

New Look _____
_____
_____

peaceful coexistence _____
_____
_____

rock 'n' roll _____
_____
_____

military-industrial complex _____
_____
_____

situation comedy _____
_____
_____

puppet governments _____
_____
_____

satellite regimes _____

## B. PHOTOGRAPHS

1.  To a viewer today, even one aware of the real repressiveness of Communist regimes, the image on the left may seem sensational and naive: Would a similar portrayal, say, of al-Qaeda or Saddam Hussein work as propaganda? What effects might such a campaign have on engendering or prosecuting acts of espionage? You can approach this exercise from the perspective that both of the Rosenbergs were guilty as charged or innocent, or that we still really do not know.

_____
_____
_____
_____
_____
_____
_____
_____
_____
_____
_____
_____
_____
_____

_____

_____

_____

_____

_____

_____

_____

_____

_____

2. In the 1950s, housing developments like this fulfilled the dreams of many American families. In the 1960s, they were widely criticized for sterile conformity, and for lacking the sense of close-knit community earlier urban neighborhoods were thought to provide. In hindsight, how did these developments improve or degrade American life? How is this experiment reflected or reversed in housing tastes today?

_____

_____

_____

_____

_____

_____

_____

_____

_____

_____

_____

_____
_____
_____
_____
_____
_____
_____
_____

3. Write a half page summarizing the long-term impact that either or both of these musicians had on American culture, social customs, politics, expectations, and economic life.

_____
_____
_____
_____
_____
_____
_____
_____
_____
_____
_____
_____
_____
_____
_____
_____

**NAME** _____  **DATE** _____

_____
_____
_____
_____
_____
_____
_____
_____

## C. VOCABULARY

containment _____
_____
_____

ideology _____
_____
_____

blacklist _____
_____
_____

Sputnik _____
_____
_____

hysteria _____
_____
_____

Tupperware _____
_____
_____

## D. INDIVIDUALS

Robert A. Taft _____
_____

George F. Kennan _____
_____

Chuck Berry _____
_____

Earl Tupper _____
_____

Paul Robeson _____

_____

Dean Acheson _____

_____

Julius Rosenberg _____

_____

Ethel Rosenberg _____

_____

Whittaker Chambers _____

_____

Alger Hiss _____

_____

Elvis Presley _____

_____

Nikita Khrushchev _____

_____

Richard Nixon _____

_____

Berry Gordy, Jr. _____

_____

Harry Truman _____

_____

Thomas E. Dewey _____

_____

Benjamin Spock _____

_____

_____

Dwight D. Eisenhower _____

_____

_____

Strom Thurmond _____

_____

_____

Jack Kerouac _____

_____

_____

John Foster Dulles _____

_____

_____

William J. Levitt _____

_____

_____

Matthew Ridgway _____

_____

_____

Allen Ginsberg _____

_____

_____

Henry A. Wallace _____

_____

_____

Joseph McCarthy _____

_____

_____

## E. ORGANIZATIONS

United Nations _____

_____

_____

World Health Organization _____

_____

_____

National Security Council _____

_____

_____

Central Intelligence Agency _____

_____

Warsaw Pact _____

_____

North Atlantic Treaty Organization _____

_____

Children's Crusade Against Communism _____

_____

Voice of America _____

_____

National Congress of American Indians _____

_____

GI Forum _____

_____

House Un-American Activities Committee _____

_____

Fair Employment Practices Commission _____

_____

Eightieth Congress _____

_____

States' Rights Party _____

_____

## F. FILL IN THE BLANKS.

In 1957 the Soviet Union launched a _____

called _____. Another of the same name

carried a dog named _____.

In 1960 an American _____ called the

_____ was _____ over the

U-2
other-directed
firm goals demanding work
spy plane
Soviet Union
tastes
*The Lonely Crowd*
satellite
angrily walked out

continued next page

_____. This interrupted a high level summit meeting when

_____ Nikita Khrushchev _____.

David Riesman's book _____ argues that

the nineteenth-century American mentality it describes

as _____ gave way in the twentieth to a mind

that is _____. This means that instead of centering

their lives on _____, Americans had turned in recent times

to defining themselves by _____ shared with their

friends or others.

the Soviet premier
inner-directed
Sputnik
Laika
shot down

## G. TRUE FALSE—circle one.
1. T F  The charter for the United Nations was written in San Francisco in 1945.
2. T F  UN member nations contributed military forces for two major wars: Korea from 1950 to 1953 and the Gulf War in 1991.
3. T F  The United States in 1950 supported immediate independence for all French colonies in Indochina, offering vast sums to finance liberation movements in the region.
4. T F  The Beat culture, in rebellion against what its adherents thought to be American conformity, embraced the primal energies of the American land and its cities.
5. T F  The National Association for the Advancement of Colored People fought vigorously against the Cold War anticommunism waged by Truman liberals.
6. T F  During the Cold War, critics of American institutions came to believe that liberalism would eventually accept a fundamental redistribution of political and economic power.
7. T F  Conservative isolationists considered aid to other nations, even to contain Communism, to be just another New Deal giveaway of American tax dollars.
8. T F  Many socialists and radicals preferred waging the Cold War on Truman's terms to allowing expansion of a repressive Communist system.
9. T F  A substantial portion of Communist Party members in the United States by the late 1950s were agents of the FBI.
10. T F  When a strike threatened to bring about a national emergency, railway union leaders persuaded President Truman to veto legislation authorizing the president to draft workers.
11. T F  The State Department pursued a vigorous diplomatic campaign to persuade the British government to allow Paul Robeson to return to Great Britain to sing.
12. T F  After the Taft-Hartley Act was passed, labor disputes generally resulted in wage increases that management passed on to consumers in the form of higher prices.
13. T F  President Truman tried to win back southern voters in 1948 with executive orders reaffirming racial segregation in the armed forces and in the federal civil service.
14. T F  Congress passed from Democratic to Republican control in 1946, then back to Democratic control after the 1948 election.
15. T F  After accusing the highly decorated General Ralph Zwicker of covering up subversion, Senator Joseph McCarthy began to lose power and support.
16. T F  Early in the Korean War, the North Korean army drove United Nations forces into a narrow patch of territory surrounding the port of Inchon.
17. T F  President Eisenhower remarked that since the United States already had the ability to destroy an enemy, developing additional destructive power would be pointless.
18. T F  Communist governments suppressed the flow of information from both within and outside their countries.
19. T F  Alger Hiss was convicted under the Smith Act of membership in the Communist Party and conspiracy to overthrow the United States government.

20. T  F  By 1960, about a third of the American people lived in suburbs.
21. T  F  In the 1950s, industrial workers came to outnumber clerical and other white-collar workers for the first time since agriculture ceased to be the majority occupation.

## H. MULTIPLE CHOICE—circle one or more correct answers.

1. Walter Reuther, militant leader of the United Auto Workers, wanted assurances that
   a) Communists would be allowed to run for office in federal elections.
   b) any investigation of Communists in his union would be cleared with the union leadership first.
   c) the worldwide struggle against Communism would be for democracy and not for wealth and privilege.
   d) Communists in top managerial positions at General Motors, Chrysler, and Ford would be rooted out.
   e) AFL President George Meany was not a sleeper Soviet agent.

2. The Hollywood Ten were movie script writers who
   a) pioneered anticommunist films such as *I Married a Communist.*
   b) refused to appeal to the Fifth Amendment when called before HUAC.
   c) discovered Woody Allen and boosted his acting career.
   d) refused cooperation with HUAC on the ground that its snooping amounted to an effort to frighten the film industry away from independent thinking.
   e) exposed Lucille Ball as a Communist sympathizer.

3. Paul Robeson
   a) was executive director of the NAACP.
   b) had been a Columbia Law School classmate of Thomas E. Dewey and William O. Douglas.
   c) as an actor was best known for his stage role of Othello in Shakespeare's play.
   d) sang at a Peekskill concert in 1949 sponsored by the American Legion.
   e) was invited to visit the Soviet Union by Sergei Eisenstein.

4. The Taft-Hartley Act, passed in 1947 over President Truman's veto,
   a) authorized military court-martials for anyone who participated in a strike.
   b) forbade secondary boycotts, in which workers refuse to handle goods from or for a company whose employees are on strike.
   c) prohibited the closed shop, in which only union members can be hired.
   d) modified the Thirteenth Amendment to reauthorize involuntary servitude in any industry deemed essential to national security.
   e) allowed the president to impose an eighty-day cooling-off period before any strike that might endanger the national interest.

5. The report "To Secure These Rights" presented to President Truman proposed
   a) an executive order ending racism in the federal government.
   b) designating five states to be reserved for African Americans by 1967.
   c) outlawing of racial discrimination in employment, interstate transportation, and public accommodations.
   d) desegregation of public schools "with all deliberate speed."
   e) federal protection of voting rights.

6. Presidential candidates opposing President Truman in the 1948 election included
   a) the Republican nominee, Thomas Dewey of New York.
   b) the Communist nominee, Joseph McCarthy of Wisconsin.
   c) the Dixiecrat nominee, Strom Thurmond of South Carolina.
   d) the Conservative nominee, Henry A. Wallace of Iowa.
   e) the Progressive nominee, Eugene V. Dennis of California.

122

7. Combatants in the Korean War included
   a) a corrupt, dictatorial regime governing South Korea.
   b) a Communist insurgency on the Inchon peninsula.
   c) military officers funded by the Central Intelligence Agency.
   d) a ruthless and brutal Communist government in North Korea.
   e) a brigade of mercenaries commanded by General Douglas MacArthur.

8. In the 1950s the CIA arranged to overthrow
   a) Francisco Franco's government in Spain, which had earlier received Nazi aid.
   b) the elected premier of Iran, Mohammed Mossadegh, replaced by a monarchy.
   c) Poland's Communist government, opposed by exiles from Chicago.
   d) the brutal dictatorship of Fulgencio Batista in Cuba.
   e) the elected president of Guatemala, replaced by a military dictatorship.

9. In the 1950s, the possibility of nuclear warfare inspired
   a) air raid drills in which school children took shelter under desks and tables.
   b) movies about future earths or other planets ruined by atomic wars.
   c) government leaflets explaining how to dig survival shelters in back yards.
   d) a massive peace movement in the United States that nearly took over one or the other political party.
   e) a policy relying on nuclear capability to allow cuts in other military spending.

10. Beginning in 1950, the Truman administration gave vast sums of money to France to
    a) compensate a wartime ally for voluntarily giving up its colonial empire.
    b) rebuild the Maginot Line, which the French military continued to believe might work against a German invasion.
    c) finance an attempt to retain its colonial empire in Indochina, including Vietnam.
    d) liquidate the Algerian independence movement with savage counterinsurgency.

11. President Eisenhower's policy toward Asia included
    a) rearming Japan to begin war against the Soviet Union in Siberia.
    b) protecting Chiang Kai-shek on Taiwan from direct Communist attack.
    c) financing anticommunist guerrillas in Mongolia.
    d) ordering General Douglas MacArthur to invade the Chinese mainland.
    e) refusing American air support to French forces at Dienbienphu in Vietnam.

12. The development of American suburbs resulted in
    a) loss of tax revenues to cities where a great number of suburban residents still worked.
    b) close-knit ethnic communities grouped around a common religious faith.
    c) opportunity for many veterans and newlyweds to own their own home.
    d) loosening of ties to urban neighborhoods, village homes, and family farmsteads.
    e) an end to racially segregated patterns in housing and home ownership.

13. Traditional gender roles in the 1950s followed a pattern calling for
    a) women to get jobs while a man was allowed to hang around any woman who could support him.
    b) a mother to remain at home, not to uphold traditional feminine virtues but as a professional operating modern appliances, and a student of proper diet.
    c) men to be the primary family breadwinner, although women might have lower paying jobs as telephone operators, secretaries, or waitresses.
    d) people to marry early, recognizing that divorce was always available if the marriage was imperfect.
    e) husbands and wives to share responsibilities for supervising homework, preparing meals, washing dishes, and bathing children.

14. Who observed that every weapon means money taken from the cold and hungry?
   a) Adlai Stevenson
   b) Mao Zedong
   c) Joseph McCarthy
   d) Dwight Eisenhower
   e) John L. Lewis

15. In the 1950s "duck and cover" was a common phrase referring to
   a) a rock and roll dance made popular by Bill Halley and the Comets.
   b) a method for quick meal preparation introduced at Tupperware parties.
   c) an animated adventure produced by Walt Disney.
   d) the act of children lying down and pulling clothing over exposed skin in the event of a nuclear attack.
   e) Joseph McCarthy's political posture when he could not back up his accusations.

## I. ESSAY QUESTIONS OR ORAL REPORTS

1. Look up the basic tenets of the fascist and Nazi ideologies, on the one hand, and of Communist ideology on the other. What sort of people were attracted to each? What goals motivated them? During the twentieth century, how did Communism and fascism resemble each other in actual governance of nations? How did they differ?

2. Document the relationship between the right-wing opposition to international alliances for the defeat of Communism and the campaigns of right-wingers in search of Communists within American life. Select five to ten individuals who led anticommunist crusades within the nation, and examine their own positions toward NATO, the United Nations, and foreign aid.

3. Draw up a general description of the course of the Korean War. Why did the North Korean army have such quick success at the beginning? Why did the counterattack at Inchon reverse the balance of power so thoroughly? On what basis did MacArthur presume that China would not intervene, and why did China intervene? Why did the American and other armies have to retreat, and how did they eventually steady their lines?

4. Read *The Lonely Crowd* or *The Organization Man*, each claiming to describe the state of mind and culture within the American middle classes in the years after the end of the Second World War. Do you think that the author was perceptive about his own period? In any case, demonstrate that the thesis of the book of your choice is or is not applicable also to subsequent decades.

5. Document the causes of the wave of labor strikes in 1946 and 1947. In what ways did they, or did they not, accomplish their objectives, and how did they influence public perceptions of labor unions and strengthen or weaken the union movement in subsequent years?

# Politics Takes to the Streets

## 24

## A. TERMS

civil disobedience _____
_____
_____

white supremacy _____
_____
_____

poll tax _____
_____
_____

participatory democracy _____
_____
_____

Freedom Summer _____
_____
_____

black power _____
_____
_____

termination (of Indian tribal status) _____
_____
_____

voter registration _____
_____
_____

## B. PHOTOGRAPHS

1. Study the picture on the next page and imagine someone who is eating at this lunch counter when the events pictured begin to happen. Write a brief description of how such a person might respond.

_____

_____

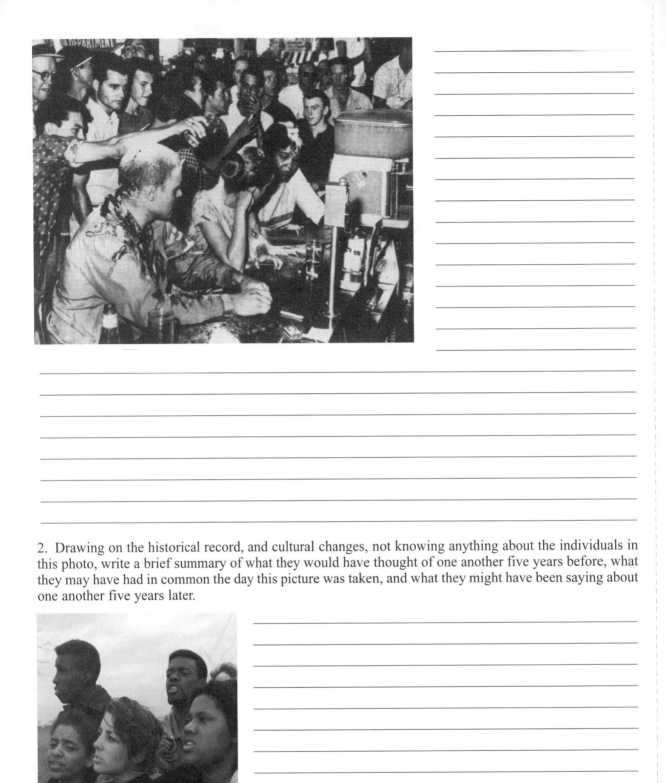

2.  Drawing on the historical record, and cultural changes, not knowing anything about the individuals in this photo, write a brief summary of what they would have thought of one another five years before, what they may have had in common the day this picture was taken, and what they might have been saying about one another five years later.

_____
_____
_____
_____
_____
_____
_____
_____

## C. VOCABULARY

nonviolence _____
_____
_____

subjugation _____
_____
_____

segregation _____
_____
_____

integration _____
_____
_____

bigotry _____
_____
_____

## D. INDIVIDUALS

Oliver Brown _____
_____
_____

Rosa Parks _____
_____
_____

Martin Luther King, Jr. _____
_____
_____

Jo Ann Robinson _____
_____
_____

Orval Faubus _____
_____
_____

James Meredith _____

_____

Autherine Lucy _____

_____

Charlayne Hunter-Gault _____

_____

Ross Barnett _____

_____

Robert Kennedy _____

_____

George Wallace _____

_____

Jimmy Lee Jackson _____

_____

James Reeb _____

_____

Viola Liuzzo _____

_____

Clark Kerr _____

_____

Mario Savio _____

_____

Robert Parris Moses _____

_____

Fannie Lou Hamer _____

_____

Medgar Evers _____
_____
_____

James Chaney _____
_____
_____

Michael Schwerner _____
_____
_____

Stokely Carmichael _____
_____
_____

Andrew Goodman _____
_____
_____

Malcolm X _____
_____
_____

Huey P. Newton _____
_____
_____

Lyndon Johnson _____
_____
_____

Bobby Seale _____
_____
_____

César Chávez _____
_____
_____

Dolores Huerta _____
_____
_____

Reies López Tijerina _____
_____
_____

"Bull" Connor _____
_____
_____

# E. ORGANIZATIONS AND PROJECTS

Southern Christian Leadership Conference _____

_____

Congress of Racial Equality _____

_____

Alliance for Progress _____

_____

Peace Corps _____

_____

Special Forces _____

_____

Students for a Democratic Society _____

_____

Student Nonviolent Coordinating Committee _____

_____

Black Panther Party for Self Defense _____

_____

American Indian Movement _____

_____

National Farm Workers Association _____

_____

La Alianza (Federal de Mercedes) _____

_____

Economic Research and Action Project _____

_____

Mississippi Freedom Democratic Party _____

_____

NAME _____  DATE _____

## F. TRUE FALSE—circle one.

1. T F Governor Orval Faubus of Arkansas called out his state's National Guard to protect black students entering Little Rock High School for the first time.
2. T F Mobs in Alabama burned Greyhound buses to protest the refusal of white drivers to allow black passengers to board.
3. T F In 1961 the Interstate Commerce Commission banned segregation in interstate travel.
4. T F The Kennedy administration promised not to interfere in the arrest of Freedom Riders in Mississippi if their physical safety was guaranteed.
5. T F The repressive regime of Fidel Castro in Cuba cooperated with Moscow even as it improved the lives of Cubans.
6. T F The Cuban Missile Crisis was resolved by Soviet consent to remove nuclear weapons from Cuba and agreement by the United States not to invade the island.
7. T F In 1961 the Democratic Party, which had relied on white southern voters as its mainstay, remained uneasy about pressing racial issues.
8. T F The Manpower Development Act tried to increase the number of minimum-wage jobs by subsidizing temporary employment agencies with a national customer base.
9. T F Liberalism practiced by the Kennedy and Johnson administrations looked to create something like a commonwealth of workers rather than to make permanent an underclass depending on welfare payments.
10. T F President Kennedy delivered a speech at American University in 1963 calling for an end to the Cold War.
11. T F The Nation of Islam, led by Elijah Muhammad, known as the Black Muslims, introduced African Americans to the Shi'ite branch of the Islamic faith.
12. T F Malcolm X's pilgrimage to Mecca in 1964 introduced him to an Islam that embraced people of all races.
13. T F Head Start and Legal Services were among the most enduring programs begun under the Economic Opportunity Act of 1964.
14. T F In becoming militant and confrontational, some federally-funded community action groups made the poverty program an easy political target.
15. T F Local officials attempting to prevent African Americans from voting in the United States in the twentieth century were acting in accordance with the authority the Constitution leaves to the states.
16. T F Mobs at the University of Mississippi threatened the lives of federal marshals sent to enforce the registration of James Meredith as a student, and federal troops had to be sent in.
17. T F Police in Selma, Alabama, turned out in 1965 to protect from white mobs and state troopers the marchers campaigning to register African American voters.
18. T F The March on Washington in 1963 was inspired and planned by the Reverend Martin Luther King, Jr.
19. T F The Voting Rights Act of 1965 sent federal registrars into states that had systematically obstructed registration of black voters.
20. T F The 1960 presidential election between John F. Kennedy and Richard Nixon presented voters with sharp contrasts in ideology and goals for American policy.
21. T F Liberals, in conflict with institutions of power and production, criticized the Kennedy tax cut of 1964, charging that it would please wealthy taxpayers and business interests.

## G. MULTIPLE CHOICE—circle one or more correct answers.

1. The Montgomery bus boycott began when
   a) bus drivers went on strike and asked for public support.
   b) Ku Klux Klan chapters protested desegregation of public schools.
   c) a white bus driver ordered disruptive black teenagers to sit toward the front.
   d) Rosa Parks was arrested for refusing to yield her seat to a white passenger.
   e) a black bus driver ordered disruptive white teenagers to sit toward the front.

2. Oliver Brown, the plaintiff in *Brown* v. *Board of Education*, was concerned that
   a) his daughter was sent to a segregated school miles away from her home.
   b) the white school his daughter was sent to did not begin the day with a prayer.
   c) there was a neighborhood school down the street reserved for white students only.
   d) his daughter had to walk through hostile white neighborhoods to get to school.
   e) his daughter needed the supportive community of an all-black school.

3. The lunch counter sit-in in Greensboro, North Carolina, began on February 1, 1960,
   a) at a part of a Woolworth's lunch counter reserved for white customers only.
   b) when volunteers from New York City arrived to lead the protest.
   c) after federal troops sealed off the downtown area.
   d) and had four African American students in a circle reciting the Lord's Prayer after that day's demonstration.
   e) and grew from four people to sixty to three hundred in five days.

4. Between 1960 and 1966 black voter registration more than doubled in
   a) Alabama, Tennessee, Arkansas, and Missouri.
   b) Texas, North Carolina, Tennessee, and Florida.
   c) Georgia, Louisiana, Virginia, and Kentucky.
   d) Mississippi, Alabama, South Carolina, and Virginia.
   e) Ohio, Mississippi, Arkansas, and California.

5. Kennedy's presidential election was unique because
   a) he was the first president to win in an election in which a vote count was disputed.
   b) he was the youngest president ever elected.
   c) no Democrat who won the West Virginia primary had ever become president.
   d) he was the first president to have graduated from Harvard.
   e) he was the first Roman Catholic ever elected president.

6. The invasion of Cuba at the Bay of Pigs in 1961 failed because
   a) the commanders of the invasion force were secretly working for Fidel Castro.
   b) radio broadcasts in support of the invasion were all in English.
   c) the shallow landing zone dotted with coral reefs was poorly chosen.
   d) a mistake in communication led Florida state police to arrest half the invasion force.
   e) people in Cuba did not rise up against Castro when the invaders landed.

7. When major steel companies ("Big Steel") raised prices in 1962, President Kennedy
   a) announced that the government had no authority to intervene in the steel market.
   b) threatened antitrust action and a tax audit of the companies involved.
   c) offered subsidies to develop steel industries in Europe and Asia.
   d) shifted government contracts to steel companies that had not raised prices.
   e) asked Congress for authority to nationalize the steel industry.

8. The Free Speech Movement at the University of California at Berkeley in 1963 and 1964
   a) was inspired and led by students seeking freedom to use obscenities in public.
   b) began when the university administration banned solicitation on campus for political causes, including the setting up of tables and the distribution of literature.
   c) rose to prominence after recruitment for the civil rights movement occurred in defiance of the ban on political solicitation.
   d) had a corps of student leaders returned from a summer work and education program in Havana, Cuba.
   e) led to occupation of the administration building, named Sproul Hall, which police took hours to clear, making hundreds of arrests.

9. Programs inspired under the Economic Opportunity Act of 1964 and directed by Sargent Shriver included
   a) confiscation of the property of large corporations to create worker cooperatives.
   b) subsidies to the Black Panthers and SDS to purchase guns and make bombs.
   c) the Job Corps, designed to bring unemployed young people into camps to learn work skills.
   d) the Community Action Program, giving money to neighborhood and Indian reservation groups for education and training.
   e) Legal Services, providing the poor with free legal assistance.

10. When a federal court ordered integration of public schools in Little Rock, Arkansas,
   a) hundreds of African American students were transferred, overcrowding the high school that had been reserved for whites.
   b) Governor Orval Faubus called out his state's National Guard to obstruct integration in the name of warding off public disorder.
   c) mobs encouraged by the governor's action gathered around Central High School to threaten the handful of African American students entering the school.
   d) Martin Luther King led several months of prayer vigils and peaceful marches through downtown Little Rock.
   e) President Eisenhower placed the state's National Guard under federal authority and sent federal troops, the first use of the armed forces to defend civil rights since the end of Reconstruction after the Civil War.

11. Civil rights protests in Birmingham, Alabama, in 1963 were strengthened by
   a) a local effort to get the city's stores to hire African Americans as clerks.
   b) controversy over affirmative action programs at local universities.
   c) demands that humiliating racial signs be removed from stores.
   d) hiring policies at local steel mills that favored African Americans.
   e) mass arrests, police dogs, cattle prods, and fire hoses turned on protesters.

12. The Berlin crisis during Kennedy's administration was conditioned by
   a) agreement in 1945 that Germany should be permanently partitioned.
   b) the danger to the East German economy from the exodus of professionals from the eastern to the western zone of Berlin.
   c) a growing isolationist movement in the United States.
   d) Kennedy's commitment to keeping West Berlin out of the hands of the Communists.
   e) the unwillingness of either side to go to war over the differences.

13. President Johnson's major achievements in health care included
   a) complete socialization of all practice of medicine.
   b) universal health insurance for all Americans.
   c) Medicare, providing medical services for the elderly.
   d) eradication of tuberculosis and chicken pox.
   e) Medicaid, providing medical services for people with low incomes.

14. Black Panther Party activities from 1967 to 1972 included
   a) systematic extermination of anyone suspected of being white.
   b) armed patrols watching for police misconduct.
   c) espionage on behalf of the People's Republic of China.
   d) entering the floor of the California state assembly to present a list of demands.
   e) lobbying of Congress and state legislatures for a separate black homeland.

15. Notable turning points in the American space program included
    a) a three-day race to the moon between Russian and American spacecraft in 1967.
    b) the launching of an armed missile to destroy a Russian orbital space station in 1961.
    c) a space capsule manned by John Glenn that orbited the earth in 1962.
    d) seizure of the Van Allen radiation belt by a NATO expedition in 1965.
    e) an Apollo program spacecraft that landed two astronauts on the moon in 1969.

## H. ESSAY QUESTIONS OR ORAL REPORTS

1. Read the United States Supreme Court decisions in *Plessy* v. *Ferguson* and *Brown* v. *Board of Education of Topeka, Kansas*. (Also read the dissenting opinion in *Plessy*—the later decision was unanimous. Both decisions may be found on www.brandywinepress.com.) Outline the specific issues argued and decided in these cases. What did the two decisions have in common, and what legal reasoning and surrounding social conditions made them differ?

2. Select and analyze any major Cold War confrontation of the Kennedy administration. The Bay of Pigs, the Cuban missile crisis, and the conflict resulting in the Berlin Wall are the most obvious possibilities. Set forth and document your view of what motivated each side in the episode. What better, or worse, outcomes were a possibility? How would you have improved on the decision made by each or either side?

3. Consider the nature of poverty during the Democratic administrations of the 1960s. Do you see race as the most important cause of that poverty, as one of its causes among others, or as simply a condition that makes poverty bear harder on racial and ethnic minorities? What were the strengths and the limitations of Kennedy's efforts against poverty, and Johnson's larger efforts? Did either president consider a major redistribution of power and wealth?

4. Develop your own analysis of the reasons that the civil rights movement fragmented after 1964. What proposals can you draw from this history for resolving outstanding racial issues today?

5. Evaluate the effects of the Peace Corps on some of the countries to which volunteers were sent. What specific improvements were delivered? How were the economics and demographics of each country affected in the long run? As an alternative topic, look at a specific group of volunteers—perhaps the first year's crop—and see what economic classes of people it contained, the motives the applicants stated, and their conduct in their assignments.

6. Read Michael Harrington's *The Other America* and two books of your choice on poverty. How do the books agree or disagree? Enter into the discussion your own appraisal of the arguments within the books and your view of the subject as a whole.

7. Why did SNCC, SDS, and the Black Panther Party not maintain an enduring presence in the politics of the United States? Why did they not become, as did the labor union movement, a permanent basis of power?

8. Explain why the memory of President Kennedy has gained a lasting place in American politics and culture. Was it simply the fact of his being killed in office? Did it grow out of real substance in his administration, or the public image he cast and a sense of expectations that he evoked? Was he a product of changing times, or did his presidency change the times?

_____

_____

_____

_____

_____

# Vietnam— The Longest War

# 25

## A. TERMS

guerrilla warfare _____

_____

Vietnamization _____

_____

urban machine politics _____

_____

American military advisers _____

_____

national liberation _____

_____

## B. PHOTOGRAPHS

1. Develop your own analysis of this widely publicized incident. Find facts surrounding the shooting, General Loan's reputation and history, and the situation in the city of Hué at the time. Apply the rules of war, the American code of military justice, and any other legal or ethical considerations, as well as the practical impact on public opinion, the rationale for the presence of American troops in Vietnam, and military necessity.

_____

_____

_____

_____

_____

_____

2. What did use of the word "Revolution" mean in this setting? Was there a revolution, or attempt at one? What did the students carrying this banner have in mind? Were they mistaken one way or another? Could a revolution have resolved the concrete problems these students addressed?

_____
_____
_____
_____
_____
_____
_____
_____
_____
_____
_____
_____
_____
_____
_____
_____
_____
_____
_____

## C. VOCABULARY

dilemma _____
_____
_____

coup (or coup d'état) _____
_____
_____

counterculture _____
_____
_____

opportunism _____
_____
_____

napalm _____
_____
_____

self-immolation _____
_____
_____

politicos _____
_____
_____

defectors _____

_____

_____

technocrat _____

_____

_____

defoliants _____

_____

_____

escalation _____

_____

_____

## D. INDIVIDUALS

Maxwell Taylor _____

_____

Ho Chi Minh _____

_____

Thich Quang Duc _____

_____

Dean Rusk _____

_____

Robert McNamara _____

_____

Eugene McCarthy _____

_____

Barry Goldwater _____

_____

Richard J. Daley _____

_____

Abbie Hoffman _____

_____

Norodom Sihanouk _____
_____
_____

William Sloan Coffin _____
_____
_____

Charles de Gaulle (on Vietnam) _____
_____
_____

Ngo Dinh Diem _____
_____
_____

Jerry Rubin _____
_____
_____

William Calley _____
_____
_____

William Westmoreland _____
_____
_____

Vo Nguyen Giap _____
_____
_____

Nguyen Cao Ky _____
_____
_____

Mark Rudd _____
_____
_____

Hubert Humphrey _____
_____
_____

Nguyen Van Thieu _____
_____
_____

Daniel and Philip Berrigan _____
_____
_____

Richard Nixon (and Vietnam) _____

_____

_____

## E. ORGANIZATIONS

Institute for Defense Analysis _____

_____

_____

Youth International Party _____

_____

_____

Mobilization to End the War in Vietnam _____

_____

_____

## F. MATCHING For each event, or Vietnam War battle, listed at the left, draw a line connecting it to its description on the right.

| | |
|---|---|
| Dien Bien Phu | massacre of Vietnamese peasants by American troops in 1968 |
| Jackson State University | Johnson expected major United States victory here |
| My Lai | first major bombing by Americans in Vietnam |
| Woodstock | California rock festival where a spectator was killed |
| Khe Sanh | students killed by police gunfire in 1970 |
| Gulf of Tonkin | American base hit by effective guerrilla attacks in 1965 |
| Pleiku | National Guard wounded twelve students and killed four |
| Altamont | first major rock festival regarded by some as transforming |
| Kent State University | led Congress to give president blank check to wage war |
| Rolling Thunder | battle that ended French colonial rule in Vietnam |

## G. TRUE FALSE—circle one.

1. T  F  According to the domino theory, if one Asian country fell to Communist rule, a chain of Communist victories in neighboring countries would follow.

2. T  F  French forces returned to Indochina after the Japanese surrender in World War II to carry out a United Nations mandate to prepare nations there for independence.

3. T  F  Upon declaring Vietnam's independence from France after World War II, Ho Chi Minh sought American support and offered use of a naval base to the United States.

4. T  F  South Vietnam's population, about eighty percent Roman Catholic, welcomed rule by Ngo Dinh Diem, afraid that the Buddhist majority in the north would discriminate against them.

5. T  F  Americans accepted working with leaders like Nguyen Cao Ky and Nguyen Van Thieu because Vietcong generals were known to admire Hitler and Mussolini.

6. T  F  Ngo Dinh Diem, with American support, refused to hold elections scheduled for 1956 in Vietnam since there was no doubt that Ho Chi Minh would have won.

7. T  F  American soldiers in Vietnam found it impossible to distinguish South Vietnamese civilians, who they were sent to defend, from Vietcong they were sent to fight.

8. T  F  Liberal administrations in Washington convinced themselves that they were sending American soldiers to fight for a more democratic Vietnam.

9. T  F  Early campus teach-ins against the Vietnam War attracted a few hundred politically active students, but were largely ignored by everyone else.

10. T  F  Robert Kennedy was assassinated by an unemployed laborer whose patriotism was outraged by Kennedy's opposition to continuing the war in Vietnam.

11. T  F  Reassured by the capacity of American forces to protect them from Communists, villagers at My Lai refused to provide any further aid to the Vietcong after 1968.

12. T  F  In 1967 Martin Luther King, Jr., participated in an anti-Vietnam War rally in New York City.

13. T  F  Hubert Humphrey collected a majority of 1968 Democratic convention delegates from states where they were selected by party leaders, not by primary elections.

14. T  F  Chicago Eight defendants charged with inciting to riot at the 1968 Democratic National Convention were convicted and sentenced to life in prison without parole.

15. T  F  Almost half of the 58,000 American deaths in Vietnam occurred after Richard Nixon became president and commander-in-chief.

16. T  F  General Douglas MacArthur advised President Kennedy it would be best to make a substantial commitment of American soldiers to a land war in Vietnam.

17. T  F  George Wallace ran for president in 1968 appealing to a coalition of newly enfranchised southern black voters, northern opponents of school integration, and apolitical hippies.

18. T  F  Many liberals were alienated from Hubert Humphrey's candidacy for president in 1968.

19. T  F  Conservatives cast Hubert Humphrey, the Democratic candidate, as representative of liberalism, radicalism, drugs, and anti-Americanism.

## H. MULTIPLE CHOICE—circle one or more correct answers.

1. Nations that have tried to impose themselves militarily on Vietnam in the last thousand years include
   a) Germany.    b) France.    c) the United States.    d) China.    e) Spain.

2. The battle of Dien Bien Phu was a turning point for Vietnam because
   a) Communists in the United States State Department delivered French occupation forces into the hands of Communist insurgents.
   b) Emperor Bao Dai led a heroic nationalist resistance to the Viet Minh, even after regular French army soldiers had surrendered.
   c) a supposedly impregnable French military position in a supposed impenetrable jungle was reduced by artillery dragged to the spot.
   d) it indirectly brought about internationally supervised free and fair elections to unite the entire nation under an independent government.
   e) this devastating loss convinced the French government that further effort to retain colonial control of the country would not be worth the effort.

3. The effects of war on the life and culture of people in South Vietnam included
   a) isolation in traditional villages as the war raged around plains and cities.
   b) removal at gunpoint from ancestral villages to be confined in protected hamlets.
   c) improved agricultural methods and a growing export market for rice.
   d) separation from ancient ties to rice fields and ancestral burial grounds.
   e) death by friendly fire or indiscriminate bombing.

4. The transportation route known as the Ho Chi Minh Trail
   a) consisted of a network of ten separate good roads, concealed in the jungle.
   b) went through a series of underground tunnels running for hundreds of miles.
   c) carried substantial supplies to the south under the heaviest American bombing.
   d) sometimes ran over pontoons brought out at night where bridges were bombed.
   e) could have been shut down by one well-placed nuclear bomb.

5. The difficulties the Diem government posed for American advisers included
   a) devotion of Diem and his brother to democratic elections in the midst of a war.
   b) corruption and incompetence at all levels of the South Vietnamese government.
   c) persecution of the majority Buddhist faith by Diem, a Roman Catholic.
   d) frequent assassination of American advisers who urged immediate reforms.
   e) unfamiliarity of South Vietnamese leaders with any European language.

6. Student deferments from military selective service (2-S)
    a) were designed so college campuses would not be centers of antiwar protest.
    b) had as a rationale that well-educated people were needed in the fight against Communism.
    c) fulfilled a desire by military planners to keep radicals out of the armed forces.
    d) kept many children of affluent families out of military service.
    e) angered Americans of less privileged classes who made up most of the military.

7. Polls and other sources indicate that the attitude of Americans toward the Vietnam War
    a) was largely favorable from 1965 to 1966.
    b) never manifested much support for sending soldiers to Southeast Asia.
    c) changed by the summer of 1967, when less than half the public was supportive.
    d) produced a wave of sympathy for Communist regimes all over the world.
    e) turned toward withdrawal after the Tet offensive in 1968.

8. American responses to the My Lai massacre included
    a) huge patriotic rallies demanding occupation of all of Vietnam at any cost.
    b) the court martial and conviction of Lieutenant William Calley.
    c) admiration by some Americans who treated as heroes the officers who had ordered the killing.
    d) yellow ribbons in cities across America honoring the massacred villagers.
    e) President Nixon's parole of Calley from a long sentence.

9. When Yippies threw dollar bills onto the floor of the New York Stock Exchange,
    a) they were arrested by federal marshals for economic sabotage.
    b) the *Wall Street Journal* editorialized that there was hope for Jerry Rubin.
    c) indictments were filed against them for distributing pornography.
    d) stock traders on the floor scrambled to pick up the money.
    e) presidential candidates agreed to refuse campaign donations from stockbrokers.

10. Actions on the part of radical college students in the late 1960s included
    a) a demand that Columbia University withdraw from the Institute for Defense Analysis, a group of universities engaged in weapons research.
    b) the allocation among Harvard University students of a portion of their fees to buy minesweepers for the Democratic Republic of Vietnam.
    c) support by Columbia University students of a protest by Harlem residents of the building of a segregated gym on mutually adjacent land.
    d) African American students at Cornell University arming themselves and seizing a building to demand a separatist black studies program.
    e) students at the universities of Wisconsin and Michigan proposing that anyone bringing a stereo on campus pay a tax to support Black Panther food programs.

11. President Johnson's decision not to run for reelection in 1968 was because
    a) he foresaw that the Vietnam War was lost and did not want to preside over the end.
    b) the Johnson slate barely won more New Hampshire primary votes than Eugene McCarthy's.
    c) Hubert Humphrey was eager to run and urged Johnson to step aside.
    d) he wanted to concentrate not on electoral politics but on bringing the war to an end.
    e) Robert Kennedy, a formidable campaigner, had also entered the race.

12. Fighting along the border with Vietnam engulfed much of Cambodia in 1970 after
    a) President Sihanouk was overthrown in a coup supported by the CIA.
    b) North Vietnam invaded the country to end the rule of the Khmer Rouge.
    c) National Guard troops were airlifted to Phnom Penh to hunt for guerrillas.
    d) a large South Vietnamese and American force invaded the country.
    e) Pol Pot refused to hold scheduled elections and Sihanouk rebelled against him.

13. By the time Nixon became president, it was clear that in Vietnam
    a) United States forces were on the verge of winning an overwhelming victory.
    b) North Vietnamese armies could not win a military triumph against the United States as they had over the French at Dien Bien Phu.
    c) the Saigon government and its American allies were not going to crush the Vietcong or the North Vietnamese troops fighting at their side.
    d) Buddhist fundamentalists would take over both halves of the nation unless the war was quickly settled.
    e) a bloodless show of force in Cambodia was the key to flanking the Ho Chi Minh Trail and restoring peace to the entire region.

14. The counterculture in America became defined by
    a) turning out millions of people for demonstrations on almost any subject.
    b) small groups of men and women sharing an apartment or farmhouse commune.
    c) evolution into well armed, drug-dealing street gangs amassing great wealth.
    d) experimentation with mind-altering drugs.
    e) the practice of farming or handicrafts, working with wood, clay, and thread.

15. In disagreements between liberal and conservative approaches to the Cold War,
    a) conservatives were initially less dedicated to paying for a global strategy of containment of Communism than liberals were.
    b) conservative spokesmen proclaimed and liberals rejected a willingness to go anywhere, pay any price, bear any burden, meet any hardship to fight for freedom around the world.
    c) liberals sought from the beginning to avoid military confrontation and to compromise with Communist insurgency anywhere it appeared.
    d) liberals recognized more distinctions than did conservatives among different kinds of Communism, local peasant radicalism, and struggles for national liberation.
    e) liberals were never willing to accept any accommodation with brutal military regimes in order to advance the global fight against Communism.

## I. ESSAY QUESTIONS OR ORAL REPORTS

1. Demonstrate how the United States could have won the Vietnam War, or why the war was unwinnable and at what point the United States should have recognized that and withdrawn. Take into consideration the character of the individuals who led South Vietnamese governments and evidence of how military operations swayed the loyalty of people in South Vietnam. Also study at what points in the war increasing numbers of Americans came to oppose the government's policy and what the demography of opposition was.

2. Study the intent and actual results of the strategic hamlet program in South Vietnam. Evaluate the military benefits and costs of the system. Also examine the vision of a series of self-governing social-democratic communities freed from traditional landlords as well as Communist guerrillas. Did this system meet any of its goals? What would have been necessary to make it live up to its expected potential?

3. Examine the way the Vietnam War was reflected in popular culture as exemplified in Don McLean's *American Pie* album (comparing the title song to the less well known *The Grave*), Merle Haggard's *Okie from Muskogee*, John Prine's *Take the Star Out Of the Window* and *Sam Stone*, the John Wayne movie *Green Berets*, Sergeant Barry Sadler's *Ballad of the Green Berets*, and Arlo Guthrie's *Alice's Restaurant*. What sectors of American society did these arise from or appeal to?

4. Compare with the present volunteer recruitment the Selective Service system in use from the Korean to the end of the Vietnam War. Identify egalitarian features of each, and ways in which

each system distributes the sacrifices of military service among different strata of American society. How does each allow for individual conscience to interact with government policy? How does each make government policy more or less responsive to the political wishes of the civilian population? Would you recommend any reforms or alternative systems for keeping military units fully staffed?

5. Trace the real impact, if any, of the counterculture on American life. What portion of the population did it actually sweep up or influence? What regions and demographic groups did countercultural individuals come from? Look for ways that cultural sectors hostile to radical and communal styles were nonetheless influenced: the popularity, for example, of long shaggy hair and marijuana in southern and country life. Has the nation simply rejected the counterculture or subtly absorbed it? Do you find instances of members of the counterculture who remain true to its styles and convictions (possibly among older computer tekkies and programmers who find in their work the independence and privacy of skill they earlier sought in farming or the crafts)? Do you find others who today would be lost without a business suit?

6. How did the student left of the late 1960s differ from the traditional socialist and Communist movements of the previous century? Some activists sought to move from a student base into more traditional working-class communities: why did they fail to generate a powerful political movement? How does the situation differ from that of the early 1900s, when the Socialist Party had a popular base, and the 1930s, when the Communist Party had a presence in the union movement? Why were most Americans unwilling to re-create the same kind of movements?

# Testing the Reach of Power

## 26

## A. TERMS

identity politics _____
_____
_____

equal rights amendment _____
_____
_____

affirmative action _____
_____
_____

nonaligned nations _____
_____
_____

global strategy _____
_____
_____

New Federalism _____
_____
_____

stagflation _____
_____
_____

culture of dependence _____
_____
_____

human rights _____
_____
_____

Middle Americans _____
_____
_____

Sunbelt _____

_____

supply-side economics _____

_____

_____

## B. PHOTOGRAPHS

Richard Nixon was a president whose opponents detested him, whose supporters admired him, and who rose or fell by the impression he made at different times on everyone else. For each of these photos, write a commentary from the viewpoint of an admirer, of a critic, and of an American with no consistent strong feelings about the man one way or the other.

_____

_____

_____

_____

_____

_____

_____

_____

_____

_____

_____

_____

_____

_____

_____

_____

**NAME** _____  **DATE** _____

_____
_____
_____
_____
_____
_____
_____
_____
_____
_____
_____

## C. VOCABULARY

Watergate _____
_____

feminism _____
_____

détente _____
_____

deregulation _____
_____

authoritarian _____
_____

impeachment _____
_____

underclass _____
_____

## D. INDIVIDUALS

G. Gordon Liddy _____
_____

Daniel Ellsberg _____
_____
_____

E. Howard Hunt _____

_____

James McCord _____

_____

Jeb Stuart Magruder _____

_____

Jimmy Carter _____

_____

John Sirica _____

_____

Sam Ervin _____

_____

Salvador Allende _____

_____

Betty Friedan _____

_____

John Dean _____

_____

John Erlichman _____

_____

George McGovern _____

_____

Anita Hill _____

_____

Henry Kissinger _____

_____

Mikhail Gorbachev _____

Ronald Reagan _____

Augusto Pinochet _____

Gerald Ford _____

Ayatollah Ruhollah Khomeini _____

H. R. Haldeman _____

Manuel Noriega _____

Elliot Richardson _____

Clarence Thomas _____

Archibald Cox _____

George Herbert Walker Bush _____

## E. ORGANIZATIONS

Committee to Re-Elect the President (CREEP) _____

National Organization for Women (NOW) _____

_____

_____

La Raza Unida Party (LRU or RUP) _____

_____

_____

United Farm Workers of America (UFW) _____

_____

_____

Organization of Petroleum Exporting Countries (OPEC) _____

_____

_____

Professional Air Traffic Controllers Organization (PATCO) _____

_____

_____

## F. TRUE FALSE—circle one.

1. T F In 1969 the Redstockings advocated that all customary forms and relations between men and women should be abandoned.

2. T F The Nixon administration used the CIA to bring about the overthrow of Salvador Allende's elected leftist government in Chile in 1973.

3. T F President Nixon used the FBI to thwart a covert CIA investigation into the Watergate scandal and its ties to his 1972 reelection campaign.

4. T F In 1972 Democrats who had supported Johnson's conduct of the Vietnam War seized control of the national party from civil rights and antiwar forces.

5. T F Carter's desire to govern by moral principle gave him a powerful edge for reelection among Americans seeking spiritual leadership in government.

6. T F Nixon believed that anyone, black or white, who was not a Middle American should become one.

7. T F The spirit of liberation that gave hope to black, feminist, and antiwar movements took energy from an expansive economy, which turned downward in the 1970s.

8. T F Prior to passage of the McCarran Act in 1952, federal immigration law prohibited most immigration from Asia.

9. T F Lacking authorization from the United Nations Security Council to use force against Iraq, President George Herbert Walker Bush ordered American forces to retake Kuwait anyway.

10. T F Determination of the Reagan administration to project American strength in the world clashed with unwillingness to demand actual sacrifice from the American people.

11. T F In 1989, the tanker *Exxon Valdez* was sent to Alaskan waters to scoop up millions of gallons of oil seeping into the sea from natural vents along the coast.

12. T F The Union of Soviet Socialist Republics ceased to exist when Boris Yeltsin led a successful military coup, which non-Russian republics refused to accept.

13. T F Breaking with traditional conservative frugality, the Reagan administration adopted deficit spending, cutting taxes while borrowing money for increased military spending.

14. T F Programs such as food stamps for low-income families and free school lunches were expanded under Reagan in accordance with supply-side economic theories.

15. T F The Reagan administration refuted liberal claims that there was a "missile gap" between the United States and the USSR, thereby saving tax money by cutting military spending.

16. T F During the Gulf War, women for the first time served in combat-support positions.

17. T F President Reagan ordered an invasion of Grenada in 1983, which ousted the leftist government ostensibly in order to protect American medical students at a school on the island.

**156**

18. T F James Watt as secretary of the interior wanted offshore drilling for oil and gas, increased strip-mining, and encouraged industrial exploitation of resources.

## G. MULTIPLE CHOICE—circle one or more correct answers.

1. In *Roe* v. *Wade*, the United States Supreme Court ruled that
   a) all states must pass laws encouraging women to have abortions.
   b) states must leave first trimester abortion decisions up to the medical judgment of the pregnant woman's attending physician.
   c) doctors may not refuse to perform abortions for women who request it.
   d) states may prohibit third trimester abortions, except when it is necessary to preserve the life or health of the mother.
   e) states may not regulate the safety of abortion procedures in any way.

2. Many women with experience in the civil rights and antiwar movements turned to feminism in part because they had often been assigned to
   a) dangerous positions confronting police dogs.
   b) make all the administrative decisions, and get all the blame if things went wrong.
   c) serve as coffee makers and typists.
   d) handle press conferences.
   e) serve as sexual partners for male front-line soldiers of social change.

3. President Nixon and Secretary of State Kissinger projected a world of carefully arranged balances among which power blocs?
   a) the Soviet Union and the countries it dominated in eastern Europe
   b) Arabic-speaking and other Islamic nations
   c) the partnership of the United States with other anticommunist nations
   d) France, England, and their former colonies in Africa
   e) the People's Republic of China

4. Concentration of authority in the office of president was viewed in the twentieth century
   a) as an obstacle to participatory democracy by SDS members in Congress.
   b) skeptically by conservative Republican opponents of Franklin Roosevelt.
   c) from outside the United States as a welcome sign of strength and stability.
   d) with eager approval by Richard Nixon and his closest advisers.
   e) as a good way to empower state governments and reduce federal spending.

5. Jimmy Carter's campaign for president in 1976 reflected that he was
   a) committed to a feminist agenda and to weakening United States military power.
   b) an evangelical Christian, the first president to describe himself as "born-again."
   c) a Washington outsider, foreign to both liberals and the Republican establishment.
   d) ready to abandon the New Deal for a traditional southern conservative agenda.
   e) a white southerner committed to civil rights and racial reconciliation.

6. One important foreign policy triumph of the Carter administration was
   a) replacing the Shah of Iran by an elected president, Abol-Hassan Bani-Sadr.
   b) sustaining the government of Afghanistan against Islamic fundamentalists.
   c) ratification of a second Strategic Arms Limitation Treaty with the Soviet Union.
   d) a peace treaty between Israel and Egypt emerging from meetings at Camp David.
   e) replacing a pro-Communist government in Iraq with Arab nationalists.

7. After the United States embassy in Tehran was seized in 1979, and the staff held hostage,
   a) President Carter threatened to drop a nuclear bomb on Tehran or other cities unless the hostages were freed.

b) Iranian students holding the embassy demanded that the deposed Shah, then in the United States for medical treatment, be returned to Iran for trial.

c) the Soviet Union began to distribute copies of the Q'uran along with the Communist Manifesto as government-approved educational materials.

d) an unsuccessful attempt was made in the spring of 1980 to rescue the hostages when President Carter dispatched a special force by helicopter.

e) Ronald Reagan campaigned for president on a pledge to drop a nuclear bomb on Tehran or other cities unless the hostages were freed.

8. The Carter administration's commitment to human rights in foreign policy angered
   a) the Soviet Union, which correctly assumed that the policy condemned abuses there and among other Soviet allies.
   b) France, Germany, and Belgium, which wanted to keep a monopoly on the human rights issue and use it to condemn the United States.
   c) American advocates of military regimes friendly to Washington, which used torture and death squads, who could lose support due to human rights violations.
   d) Vietnam veterans sensitive to criticism of the American war effort, thinking the federal government might use them as a scapegoat.
   e) major stockholders in Nike Corporation, who foresaw the policy obstructing their plans to manufacture sporting goods at low cost in Southeast Asia.

9. Operation Desert Storm in 1991 included troops from the United States and
   a) Britain.    b) France.    c) Egypt.    d) Saudi Arabia.    e) Syria.

10. Supreme Court appointments from 1980 to 1992 included
    a) David H. Souter, Stephen Breyer, and John Paul Stevens, by George Herbert Walker Bush.
    b) Sandra Day O'Connor, Antonin Scalia, and Anthony M. Kennedy, by Ronald Reagan.
    c) Sandra Day O'Connor, Anita Hill, and Judith Ginsburg, by George Herbert Walker Bush.
    d) Antonin Scalia, Clarence Thomas, and William Rehnquist, by Ronald Reagan.
    e) David H. Souter and Clarence Thomas by George Herbert Walker Bush.

11. The war between the Sandinista government of Nicaragua and Contra rebels ended when
    a) a CIA-trained invasion force from Panama seized the capital city, Managua.
    b) the Sandinistas agreed to new elections, certain that they would win.
    c) air cover from a Soviet aircraft carrier allowed the army to decimate the Contras.
    d) George Bush and Boris Yeltsin agreed to divide Nicaragua into two zones.
    e) Violeta Barrios de Chamorro won an election against President Daniel Ortega.

12. Watergate became a common term in American politics because
    a) an audit of G. Gordon Liddy's expense accounts showed he had used Nixon reelection campaign funds to rent himself a luxury apartment.
    b) burglars supervised by members of Richard Nixon's reelection committee were caught planting bugs in the office of the Democratic National Committee.
    c) Jeb Stuart Magruder and John Dean switched their allegiance to the Democratic Party and revealed a Republican plan to bug the Democratic National Committee.
    d) reelection committee member James McCord, convinced his supervisors had deserted him, wrote a letter after the election asserting White House involvement.
    e) the House of Representatives impeached President Nixon.

13. Significant facts in what ultimately became known as gay liberation in America include
    a) during the 1950s, conservatives and liberals alike were hostile to homosexuality; liberals spread stories about homosexuality among Joseph McCarthy's staff.
    b) unexpected physical resistance by customers at Stonewall Inn, a gay bar in New York, to a police raid in 1969.

c) growing acceptance among federal courts, starting in 1975, that homosexuals should have the same legal right to marry as heterosexual couples.

d) the decision by the American Psychiatric Association in 1973 to revoke its longstanding definition of homosexuality as a mental disorder.

e) emergence of the AIDS virus, which in North America spread primarily among homosexuals before it became more common among heterosexuals as well.

14. Ronald Reagan's policies toward communism were reflected in
   a) Lieutenant Colonel Oliver North's advocacy of cooperation with Mikhail Gorbachev's reforms, in astute recognition of Soviet military weakness.
   b) his decision to lift the embargo on grain exports to the USSR, imposed by President Carter after the Soviet invasion of Afghanistan.
   c) repeated condemnation of the USSR as "an evil empire" and the "focus of evil," not only for being repressive but for being anticapitalist.
   d) efforts to curtail production of luxuries and investment in the entertainment industry, to put the entire nation on a war footing.
   e) closer relations with the People's Republic of China and extensive engagement with Mikhail Gorbachev.

15. The scandal which became known as Iran-Contra was the result of
   a) secret sales of American missiles to Iran for use in its war against Iraq, in exchange for Iranian influence to free American captives in Lebanon.
   b) reports by the CIA that Contra fighters from Nicaragua were receiving military training at secret bases in Iran.
   c) Reagan administration impatience with the Boland Amendment, which prohibited United States military aid to the Contra rebels in Nicaragua.
   d) CIA director William Casey's efforts to recruit Iranian communists to train with the Contras in Nicaragua for guerrilla warfare to overthrow the Islamic Republic.
   e) money from the illegal sale of missiles to Iran being used for the equally illegal purpose of purchasing arms for the Contras in Nicaragua.

## H. ESSAY QUESTIONS OR ORAL REPORTS

1. Critique or compare identity politics to interest-group politics. To what extent are the political interests of all individuals within a racial, ethnic, or biological group the same? Apply the same questions to the demographic categories of interest-group politics. Compare both to the benefits of loyalty to urban or rural machine politics. What basis of political association and conflict best promotes justice, equal opportunity, and economic prosperity for all?

2. Dissect Jeanne Kirkpatrick's definition of authoritarian and totalitarian regimes, Jimmy Carter's single standard on human rights, and various liberal or conservative reasons for adopting or rejecting each of these approaches. Is it possible to employ consistent moral principles in United States foreign policy?

3. Analyze United States policy toward the Tiananmen Square protests in China in 1989, Panama under Manuel Noriega, Nicaragua's Sandinista government, or the Iraqi invasion of Kuwait in 1990. For any of these episodes, document the publicized and unpublicized motives for our involvement or noninvolvement, the motivations of the governments involved, and the ultimate results for the people in the country.

4. Compare the political handling of the My Lai massacre, the Watergate scandal, Iran-Contra, and the Monica Lewinsky scandal. What laws were broken, and what damage inflicted upon the United States by each? What formal political processes were activated in response to each

scandal? How did each branch of government respond? What attitudes can be found in the general public response to these four events?

5. Explore either the military strategy or diplomatic build-up for the Gulf War of 1990 to 1991. Document facts to draw your own conclusions on the motivations of each party to the conflict (including enemies of Saddam Hussein within Iraq), why the war was conducted as it was, and what could have been done either to obtain a more enduring and positive result or to avert the conflict altogether.

6. Review the sources of energy on which the United States presently depends and trace the causes of recurrent crises in supply, from the OPEC embargo of 1973 to the electrical blackout of 2003. Criticize the responses offered by national leaders from Jimmy Carter to Dick Cheney. Outline a long-term solution to the need for a stable, secure energy supply.

NAME _____     DATE _____

# New Alignments and a New War   27

## A. TERMS

televised town meetings _____
_____
_____

North American Free Trade Agreement _____
_____
_____

ethnic cleansing _____
_____
_____

weapons of mass destruction _____
_____
_____

Y2K _____
_____
_____

unorganized militia _____
_____
_____

search engines _____
_____
_____

## B. VOCABULARY

militias _____
_____
_____

unilateralism _____
_____
_____

internet _____

_____

_____

Greens _____

_____

_____

police brutality _____

_____

_____

## C. INDIVIDUALS

Rodney King _____

_____

_____

William J. Clinton _____

_____

_____

H. Ross Perot _____

_____

_____

Newt Gingrich _____

_____

_____

Slobodan Milosevic _____

_____

_____

James Jeffords _____

_____

_____

Yasser Arafat _____

_____

_____

Randy Weaver _____

_____

_____

Monica Lewinsky _____

_____

_____

David Koresh _____

_____

_____

Timothy McVeigh _____
_____
_____

Al Gore _____
_____
_____

Osama bin Laden _____
_____
_____

Patrick Buchanan _____
_____
_____

John McCain _____
_____
_____

Ralph Nader _____
_____
_____

Ariel Sharon _____
_____
_____

Colin Powell _____
_____
_____

## D. ORGANIZATIONS

Reform Party _____
_____
_____

Democratic Leadership Council _____
_____
_____

al-Qaeda _____
_____
_____

Kosovo Liberation Army _____
_____
_____

Northern Alliance _____

_____

_____

Taliban _____

_____

_____

Columbine High School _____

_____

_____

Enron Corporation _____

_____

_____

**E. MATCHING** On the left are listed the scenes of some of the best known acts of bizarre violence in recent years. Draw a line matching each with the description of the one or more perpetrators on the right.

World Trade Center in 1993                 a drifting veteran of the Gulf War
Alfred P. Murrah Federal Building          al-Qaeda network
Columbine High School                      a group of Muslim fanatics in the United States
U S S *Cole*                               two angry students

**F. TRUE FALSE**—circle one.

1. T  F  The primary colors of human skin are determined by distinct red, yellow, brown, black, and white pigments.
2. T  F  Negro, the Spanish and Portuguese word for "black," has meant a person of strongly sub-Saharan African features.
3. T  F  In recent years, some Americans who by white supremacist definition would be defined as "Negro" have listed their ancestry more accurately as "mixed."
4. T  F  Email was invented by Samuel F.B. Morse in 1840, but did not become common in the United States until shortly after World War I.
5. T  F  The internet allows an individual alone in front of a computer to receive instant news, information, and misinformation from across the planet.
6. T  F  Only about half the eligible electorate went to the polls in the 1996 presidential election.
7. T  F  Word processing has made questions of precision far easier to deal with, although the art of composition remains complicated.
8. T  F  In the 1992 presidential election, Clinton received forty-three percent of the popular vote, Bush thirty-eight percent, and Perot the remaining nineteen percent.
9. T  F  President Clinton sought to cut the huge national debt built up under preceding Republican administrations.
10. T  F  Republicans in Congress gave President Clinton the margin of support necessary to pass the North American Free Trade Agreement, despite considerable Democratic Party opposition.
11. T  F  The FBI reported in 2000 that the rate of violent crimes had increased nineteen percent since 1999, and crimes against property were up twenty-one percent.
12. T  F  In 1977 over 1.82 million people were confined in state and federal prisons; by 1998 the figure had dropped to two hundred thousand.
13. T  F  According to one estimate, in 1992 less than one third of admissions to state prisons resulted from violent crimes.
14. T  F  Al Gore received the largest number of popular votes of any candidate in the 2000 presidential election.

**166**

15.  T   F   Al Gore received that largest number of electoral votes of any candidate in the 2000 presidential election.
16.  T   F   Ralph Nader won the electoral votes of several states, thereby throwing the final result in the electoral college to George W. Bush.
17.  T   F   One cause of resentment of the United States in predominantly Muslim areas of the world is American prosperity and comfort.
18.  T   F   After September 11, 2001, President Bush responded to outbursts of hatred toward Arab Americans and other Muslims by meeting with Muslim leaders and urging sanity.
19.  T   F   With air support from the United States and other nations, Northern Alliance troops in Afghanistan pressed southward, persuading one local leader after another to join them.
20.  T   F   Conflict between Israelis and Palestinians has made it difficult for President Bush to maintain good relations with Muslim nations, who identify the United States with Israel.
21.  T   F   Enron's stock manipulation and doctored books angered Democrats and employees, but Republicans expressed no concern.
22.  T   F   For most of his early presidency, George W. Bush had prepared for some action, including a possible military invasion, that could topple Saddam Hussein.
23.  T   F   Republican majority leader Senator Trent Lott's remarks at Senator Strom Thurmond's birthday party embarrassed Republicans by making it appear that their party is the proper home for white racists.

## G. MULTIPLE CHOICE—circle one or more correct answers.

1.  After the 2001 destruction of the World Trade Center, intelligence agencies quickly established that the attack had been the work of
    a) Ayatollah Ruhollah Khomeini and the Islamic Republic of Iran.
    b) Saddam Hussein and the Arab Socialist Republic of Iraq.
    c) Osama bin Laden and al-Qaeda.
    d) Eldridge Cleaver and the Black Liberation Army.
    e) Harun ar-Rashid and the Abbasid Caliphate of Baghdad.

2.  After Rodney King was pulled from his car by Los Angeles police on March 3, 1991,
    a) they found several loaded rifles in the trunk and a large quantity of cocaine.
    b) several officers mauled him without noticing an observer who was videotaping them.
    c) a riot spread in areas of the city.
    d) four policemen were tried in a largely white suburb and acquitted of all charges.
    e) protests and riots broke out after the trial, while King made a plea for calm.

3.  Newcomers in the late twentieth century that distinguish recent from earlier immigration include
    a) nurses from the Philippines and West Indies.
    b) accountants from the Democratic Peoples Republic of Korea.
    c) computer technicians from China.
    d) nuclear weapons specialists from Andorra and Liechtenstein.
    e) engineers and physicians from India.

4.  Which of these statements apply both to recent immigration and to earlier immigrant experience?
    a) Immigrants vote in a bloc for any political party friendly to the land of their birth.
    b) Friends and relatives provide information about their new homeland and sometimes offer a temporary place to stay.
    c) Newcomers make massive efforts to proselytize native-born Americans to adopt the religious beliefs of the immigrant community.
    d) Newly educated immigrants return to their home country to introduce American industrial methods in competition with American companies.
    e) Success in the new country generates a flow of money to provide for family members in the old country.

5. The phrase "don't ask – don't tell" introduced into the military by President Clinton
   a) meant that American soldiers captured by an enemy in combat should not ask their captors for news nor give out military information.
   b) required public information officers not to provide information to news reporters except in response to a direct question.
   c) provided a partial opening in the armed services for gays and lesbians, who would not be asked about their sexual orientation.
   d) refers to a long-standing tradition among enlisted service men and women not to inform superior officers about a fellow soldier's behavior.
   e) stipulated that any enlistees who by statement or behavior reveal themselves to be gay could be dismissed from military service.

6. Which of these statements concerning tariffs and free trade are true?
   a) Traditionally big business supported tariffs to increase profits.
   b) Tariffs have generally been opposed by unions, who promote international solidarity of all workers and consider tariffs a capitalist tool.
   c) Unions have supported tariffs, and still do so, to protect themselves against competition with ill-paid foreign labor, but the union leadership now sometimes adds that trade agreements with repressive regimes are collaboration with injustice abroad.
   d) Desiring to make use of low-paid labor pools abroad that modern means of transportation and communication have made available, many large companies now support free trade.
   e) In pressing for the North American Free Trade Agreement, Clinton argued that the pact would make possible the quick export of the nation's agricultural produce and computer technology to Canada and Mexico.

7. Welfare reform passed by Congress and signed by President Clinton in 1996
   a) promised to make welfare easier to obtain and rejected any requirement that recipients seek work or work training.
   b) limited an individual's total lifetime receipt of welfare to five years.
   c) by early indications seemed to be turning welfare clients into wage workers.
   d) virtually eliminated welfare.
   e) came into being just as the entire economy revived, and therefore was not tested for the results it could achieve in hard times with high unemployment.

8. The impeachment trial of President Clinton in 1998 and 1999
   a) resulted in conviction for perjury and obstruction of justice.
   b) turned on whether he had or had not propositioned Paula Jones.
   c) concerned charges that he had lied under oath to cover up a sexual affair.
   d) ended when a majority of the Senate found him not guilty.
   e) did not remove him from office, for less than two thirds of the Senate voted to convict.

9. Efforts by the Clinton administration to reconcile Israelis and Palestinians
   a) secured Israeli agreement to Palestinian autonomy in parts of the Gaza Strip and the West Bank of the Jordan River.
   b) was undermined by Republican hostility toward Jews in general and toward the existence of Israel in particular.
   c) obtained a public statement from the Palestine Liberation Organization recognizing the existence of Israel and foreswearing terrorism.
   d) ended in failure when Yasser Arafat was elected to head the PLO.
   e) was endangered by new clashes between Israelis and Palestinians beginning in 2000.

10. Arguments directed toward the tax cuts of 2001 claimed that
    a) the cuts were so beneficial to the rich that they would create dynasties of the wealthy, widening the gap between the rich and other Americans.
    b) a tax cut would discourage terrorism by placating antigovernment militias.

    c) the legislation would weaken the economic position of the middle class and undermine Social Security.

    d) the federal surplus was so large and the economy so booming that we could afford a tax cut.

    e) a tax cut would pull so much government spending out of the economy that depression and massive unemployment were bound to follow.

11. George W. Bush's new policy initiatives on the environment included
    a) removal of dangerous quantities of oil beneath Yellowstone National Park.
    b) ending participation in the discussions at Kyoto, Japan, concerning limits on industrial emissions.
    c) requesting congressional approval to drill for Alaska oil inside a wildlife refuge.
    d) tripling acreage of wetlands along lakes and rivers protected from development.
    e) blanket approval for clear-cutting national forests where developers planned to build cities.

12. When the Bush administration decided that it would be necessary to invade Afghanistan,
    a) the Pentagon estimated that a million American soldiers would be required.
    b) Secretary of Defense Rumsfeld said that Special Forces units alone could handle it.
    c) small elite units were deployed in aid of anti-Taliban forces in the country.
    d) traditional rivalries among Afghan clans reinforced hostility to the Taliban.
    e) many Afghans resented that al-Qaeda members from other lands could act like overlords.

13. Which of these statements would rightly describe attitudes that complicate the achievement of peace between Palestinians and Israelis?
    a) Many Palestinians want Israeli occupation of the West Bank ended immediately.
    b) A faction of Israelis insists on keeping the entire West Bank for Israel.
    c) Some Israelis and Palestinians claim exclusive right to Jerusalem.
    d) Assyrian Christians in Iraq claim a right to resettle anywhere in Palestine.

14. The collapse of the Enron Corporation led to revelations that
    a) executives and their accounting firm had known the company to be close to bankruptcy, but kept it secret to protect the value of Enron stock.
    b) Enron had been engaged in secret deals with foreign oil companies to create a consortium cornering the petroleum market.
    c) executives who knew what was coming had dumped their stock at the last minute, while employees and other stockholders lost their savings.
    d) many Wall Street stocks of other firms had become overvalued during the rise in stock prices from 1995 to 1999.
    e) excessive demands from Enron employee unions had bankrupted the company.

15. President Bush's plan to allow religious organizations more freely to receive funding for federal social programs ran into trouble from
    a) a coalition of American atheists who threatened to sue on the ground that no person who believed in God should have any part in spending any taxpayer's money.
    b) the revelation that some religious organizations being considered for funding of local social service programs insisted on denying jobs and services to homosexuals.
    c) secular liberals who feared that the plan would give organized religion too much power within government.
    d) the discovery that government officials were privately questioning the willingness of predominantly African American churches to keep proper records.
    e) religious conservatives who warned that the plan would give government too much power and influence over religion.

# H. ESSAY QUESTIONS OR ORAL REPORTS

1. Examine the origins of late twentieth-century Los Angeles street gangs of the sort that news coverage fixed on after the Rodney King beating, trials, and protests. How did they begin? How similar or dissimilar are they to gangs in some city of your choice in some earlier period you select in American history?

2. Define the present meaning of race and ethnicity in American life, or show why these concepts have no real meaning at all. For either perspective, assemble facts to support your position. Are there substantial distinctions between Hispanics and African Americans when many Hispanics are part African, while many African Americans have Spanish and Portuguese ancestors? What differences can be drawn between Mexicans and Native Americans? How many "white" and "black" Americans have Native American ancestors?

3. Develop an argument for or against private ownership of prisons. What are the benefits or harms to the public, prisoners, and their rehabilitation, and crime prevention? What have been some of the demonstrated successes, failures, or both, of privately run prisons? What kind of authority is vested in owners and employees of a private prison corporation as compared to that wielded by officials and guards of a government agency?

4. Make a short list of American Christian or Jewish ministries that condemn American life as decadent and degenerate. Then make a brief study of Muslim sects based outside the United States that condemn American life on the same grounds. Now analyze the ways in which the two sets of organizations present the same reasons for their condemnation and the ways in which they differ from each other. As an example, you might consider these questions: Does the Muslim fundamentalist insistence on the veiling of women accord with the Christian fundamentalist condemnation of sexual indulgence? Or does it derive from some specific command that would hold whether or not veiling decreases sexual temptation?

5. What has been the measurable impact of the North American Free Trade Agreement on the economies of the United States, Mexico, and Canada? How do these results compare with the promises of the officials who negotiated and ratified NAFTA, and the arguments of columnists who supported the arrangement? How do the results compare with the warnings of opponents? Has one nation benefited more than others, or at the expense of others?

6. The impeachment and trial of William J. Clinton was only the second time in American history that a president has been impeached. Richard Nixon resigned in the face of almost certain impeachment and removal from office. Compare with the charges against Clinton the charges against either Andrew Johnson or Richard Nixon. Draw conclusions about the proper use of impeachment powers.

7. Prepare a chronology of conflict between Israelis and Palestinians, beginning with the time of Jewish settlement preceding the establishment of Israel. Explore the roots of the conflict in British policy toward the Palestinian Mandate, and the roles of the monarchies of Jordan, Egypt, and Iraq. What motivated American support for Israel? Draw your own conclusions on the most just way to settle the conflict that accords with the most practical resolution.

8. Explain why voter participation has been so low in the past several American elections on the presidential and congressional levels. What demographic groups are most likely to vote, and which least likely? What is your explanation for the behavior of the most motivated groups, and that of the least motivated?

# Succeeding in College Courses

by John McClymer

## STUDYING A SUBJECT AND STUDYING FOR EXAMS

The instructor who designed your course hopes you will take advantage of the opportunity to learn about the subject. Your own objectives in taking the course could be different. You may be taking it because it fulfills some requirement for graduation or because it fits into your schedule or because it seems less objectionable than the alternative you could be taking.

In a better world, these differences between your objectives and the aims of the course would not matter. The studying you do to perform well on exams and papers would involve your learning a fair amount of the discipline. And so your grade would certify that you had indeed left the course with a more informed and thoughtful understanding of its material than you had when you entered it. In the world we must actually live in, the connection between studying a subject and studying for exams in the subject is not necessarily so clear or straightforward.

Many students manage to prepare themselves for mid-terms and finals without permanently adding to their understanding. There they sit, yellow hiliting pens in hand, plodding through the assigned chapters. Grim-faced, they underline every declarative sentence. Then they trace and retrace their tracks, trying to commit every yellowed fact to memory. As the time of the test draws near, they choke back the first faint feeling of panic by trying to guess the likeliest questions. By such tactics they may get ready for the exam but sabotage their chance of gaining any insight into the wider themes of the course.

Life does afford worse disasters. This one, however, is remediable. And this section of your workbook can help. It is designed to help you do well in the course, and to help you learn the subject in its own worth. These suggestions proceed on the proposition that the easiest and most satisfying way to succeed in a course is to learn its important themes and materials.

It makes very little sense, after all, to spend your time memorizing every possible detail. You may pick up a few points on the short-answer section of the exam, but those few points are a small reward for hours of studying. And, in the meantime, your comprehension of the depths of American literature, or your sensitivity to the wonderful diversity of biological processes, is mediocre.

Studying for exams is a poor way of learning anything. Learning a subject, to the contrary, is an excellent way of preparing for exams. Grasping the larger outlines of a topic makes possible the memorizing of the facts within them: the facts that you have expected your teacher to ask. The object of this essay is to persuade you to make some changes in the way you study.

Begin by conserving your yellow pens. All that hiliting simply lowers the resale value of the book. If you underline everything you read, you will wind up with a book of underlinings. That may bring some psychological comfort. All of that yellow does provide visible evidence that you read the material. It will not leave you with a useful guide to what to review. You have hilited too much, creating a democracy of facts. All authors, dates, and events are equally yellow. You need, more than anything else, some way of determining which are important.

The next step may prove harder. You will have to give up trying to learn by rote. A certain amount of memorizing may be unavoidable, but ultimately it is the enemy of understanding. That is because many people use it as an alternative to thinking. Have you ever wished there were a better way? Well, there is. Suppose you expect an examination to ask you about nineteenth-century New England authors and what their literary intentions were. You could take each writer separately and pound into your head information about Ralph Waldo Emerson's ideas, along with Nathaniel Hawthorne's and those of Henry David Thoreau. Or you could look at something that united them, their fascination with nature: the magnificent nature of the continent and the human nature that it mirrors. Then you might more easily remember Emerson's search for a source of inspiration within human nature, Hawthorne's grim sense of the wilderness within us, Thoreau's effort to cultivate his nature at the unspoiled edge of Walden Pond.

If you take care of the ideas, the facts will assemble themselves. That has to do with the way in which textbooks are written and courses taught. It also relates to how people learn.

No teacher or instructor pretends that the present state of knowledge, or any future state, can embrace all the facts of a subject. Even though scholars are always interested in finding new information, and in finding new ways of using information already known, each individual article, doctoral dissertation, monograph, textbook, or course of lectures represents hundreds and thousands of choices about what to include and what to omit. The information you actually encounter in a course, as a result, is there because the text authors or your teacher decided for some reason to include it. Usually the reason is that this particular bit of information helps explain or illustrate some pattern of behavior or thought. Focus on these patterns. They are what you should be thinking about.

In doing so, you will have the approval of learning theorists. They have found that while it is difficult for people to recall disconnected bits of data, it is comparatively easy to remember details of coherent stories.

Neither compulsive underlining nor prodigious memorization will help you to understand these patterns. What will? Rephrase the question: What does it mean to read and listen intelligently?

For most students, reading and listening are passive forms of behavior. They sit and wait to be told. Someone else, they expect, will provide the answers. Even worse is that they expect that someone else will provide the questions.

Letting your teacher or the authors of the text do your thinking for you leads to tedium. Passivity is boring. Yet people rarely blame themselves for being bored. It cannot be your own fault. You are only "taking" the course. Someone else is "giving" it, and so you look to the instructor to liven things up a touch. Maybe some audio-visuals or a bit of humor, you think, would make the course less dreary. These hopes are misplaced, for while humor is a blessed thing and audio-visuals have their place, it is the substance of the course that should interest you.

Boredom is almost always a self-inflicted wound. Students are bored because they expect the instructor always to be interesting when it is they who must themselves take an interest.

Taking an interest involves learning to read and listen actively. Intellectual activity begins with questions—your own questions directed, in the first instance, to yourself and then to your teacher. Why is it, you might wonder, that the United States is the only industrialized country without a comprehensive national system of health care? Why were New England authors drawn to the innocence or the mysterious evil of the wilderness in nature and the soul? How do rock strata yield their data to geologists?

You will not always find satisfactory answers. But you will have started to think about the meaning of the subject. And when you do, something quite desirable happens to all of those facts. They will take on life and become evidence, clues to the answers you are seeking. The questions will give you a rational basis for deciding which facts are important.

All of this leads directly to the question of how you should study for a course. It is too easy to assume that the sole reason why students are sometimes ill-prepared is that they did not spend enough time getting ready. This is a half-truth, and a dangerous one. It ignores the inefficiency of much reviewing itself.

How do you get ready for an exam? Do you get out your textbook and notes and pour over them again and again until the time runs out or the sheer boredom of it all crushes your good intentions? If so, then you have lots of company—a consolation of sorts. Available, on the other hand, is a better way.

Find a quiet and comfortable spot. Bring along a blank pad and something to write with. Then jot down, just as they occur to you, whatever items you can remember about the course. Do not rush yourself. And do not try, at this stage, to put things in order. Just sit there and scribble down whatever pops into your mind. After a while you will have quite a large and varied mix of facts. Then see how much of this you can put together. You do not need to write out whole sentences or paragraphs. An arrow or a word or two will frequently be enough. You are not, after all, going to hand in these scribbles. You are just collecting your thoughts. Do not be concerned if this process seems to be taking up some of the limited time you have to study. It will prove to be time well spent.

Now look over what you have written. Where are the gaps? You will find that you know a fair bit about the material just from your previous reading of the text and from listening in class. But some topics will still be obscure. Now you know what you should be studying. Why study what you already know? And here is the nub of the matter, for an intelligent review focuses on what you need to refresh your mind about.

You will doubtless have noticed that this strategy presupposes that you have read the textbook and taken good notes in class. Just what, you might wonder, are good notes? Many students think that the closer they come to transcribing the instructor's every word the better their notes are. They are mistaken, and for several reasons.

One is that unless you are an expert at shorthand, you will not succeed. Instead you will be frantically scrambling to catch up. At the end of class you will have a sore hand, a great deal of barely legible notes, and little if any idea of what the class was about.

Another reason not to attempt to transcribe lectures—taping them usually wastes time—is that you will spend much of your hour taking down information you either already know or can easily find in the textbook. How often do you need to see that Jefferson Davis was the president of the Confederacy?

The most important reason not to take down everything is that it prevents you from doing what you ought to be doing during class, listening intelligently. Your instructor is not simply transmitting information but also seeking to explain the principles of the discipline. It is these explanations you should be listening for, and your notes should concentrate on them. It is much easier to do this if you have read the relevant textbook chapters first. That way you will already know much of the information. And you will have some questions already in your mind, something to listen for. You can take notes sensibly. You can fill in explanations of points that had puzzled you, jot down unfamiliar facts, and devote most of your time to listening instead of writing. Your hand will not be sore; you will know what the class was about; and your notes will complement rather than duplicate what you already knew.

So far we have dealt mainly with the mechanics of studying—taking notes, reviewing for exams, and the like. Valuable as knowing the mechanics can be, the real secret to studying is learning how to think within the ultimate intentions and boundaries of the field. Biology is an attempt to understand the flow and self-articulation of life through its innumerable species and its ways of generation. History is a way of thinking about the human condition. Scholars of literature quarrel about the essence of their topic, but together they study the imagination of writers and the means by which words shapen and express that imagination. And so, as you learn the details of the subject and the ways those details relate to one another, think even more broadly what the field of study is all about. Think not only of a particular species, but of the innumerable new species that might come of its reproductive processes; consider both the specific causes of the Civil War and the universal motives of pride and greed and loyalty that found an occasion then; reflect not solely on the effect of nature on the New England mind but on the task of all writers who seek the exact phrase to speak their mind.

## HOW TO TAKE EXAMS

In the best of worlds examinations would hold no terrors. You would be so well prepared that no question, no matter how tricky or obscure, could shake your serene confidence. In the real world, it seems, preparation is always less than complete. "Of course," you say to yourself, "I should have studied more. But I did not. Now what?" This section will not tell you how to get A's without study, but it will suggest some practical steps that will help you earn the highest grade compatible with what you do know.

Before you begin answering any of the essay portion of the exam, look over the entire essay section. It is impossible to budget your time sensibly until you know what the whole exam looks like. And if you fail to allow enough time for each question, two things— both bad—are likely to happen. You may have to leave some questions out, including perhaps some you might have answered very effectively. How often have you muttered: "I really knew that one"? The other unhappy consequence is that you may have to rush through the last part of the exam, including questions you could have answered very well if you had left more time.

How do you budget your time effectively? The idea, after all, is to make sure that you have enough time to answer fully all the questions you do know. So the best plan is also the simplest. Answer those questions first.

Answering question #7 before #4 may seem odd at first, but you will soon enough get used to it. And you will find that, if you still run out of time, you at least have the satisfaction of knowing you are rushing through questions you could not have answered very well anyway. You will have guaranteed that you will receive the maximum credit for what you do know. Answering questions in the order of your knowledge has an immediate psychological advantage too. Most students are at least a little tense before an exam. If you answer the first several questions well, that tension will likely go away. As you relax, you will find it easier to remember names, dates, and other bits of information. If you get off to a shaky start, a simple case of pre-exam jitters can become full-scale panic. Should that happen, you may have trouble remembering your own phone number.

Let us suppose you have gotten through everything you think you know on the exam and still have some time left. What should you do? You can now try to pick up a few extra points with some judicious guessing. Trying to guess with essay questions is of little use. In all probability you will write something so vague that you will not get any credit for it anyway. You should try instead to score on the short answer section.

Some types of questions were made for shrewd guesswork. Matching columns are ideal. A process of elimination will often tell you what the answer has to be. Multiple choice questions are almost as good. Here too you can eliminate some of the possibilities. Most teachers feel obliged to give you a choice of four or five possible answers, but find it hard to come up with more than three that are plausible. So you can normally count on being able to recognize the one or two that are there just as padding. Once you have narrowed the choices to two or three, you are ready to make your educated guess. Always play your hunches, however vague. Your hunch is based on something you heard or read even if you cannot remember what it is. So go with it. Do not take your time. If you cannot think of the answer, just pick one and have done with it. Try to avoid changing answers. A number of studies show that you are more likely to change a right answer than to correct a wrong one.

Identifications are the type of short-answer question most resistant to guesswork. Don't spend much time on questions for which you have little idea of an answer, but try to come up with something better than a slapdash hunch. (This does not contradict the advice about playing hunches on multiple-choice questions. Such questions offer alternatives, one of which may tickle your memory.) You want the exam as a whole to convey what you do know. Supplying a mass of misinformation usually creates a presumption that you do not know what you are talking about even on those sections of the exam for which you really do. So be careful about wild guesses. Be prepared to present your instructor with a solid assemblage of good factual answers that will indicate that while you have achieved a critical understanding of the themes of the course, you have also respected the facts to which those themes speak.

These suggestions are not substitutes for studying. They may, however, help you get the most out of what you know. They may, that is, make the difference between a mediocre and a good grade.

## HOW TO WRITE BOOK REVIEWS

One goal of book reviews is to set forth clearly and succinctly who would benefit from reading the work in question. It follows that a good review indicates the scope of the book, identifies its point of view, summarizes its main conclusions, evaluates its use of evidence, and—where possible—compares the book with others on the subject.

You have probably written book reviews in high school or in other college courses. You may then be in danger of approaching this kind of assignment with a false sense of security. It sounds easy, after all, to write an essay of five hundred words or so. And you have written lots of other reviews. But did those other reviews concentrate clearly on the questions a good review must address? If they did not, your previous experience is not going to prove especially helpful. You may even have developed some bad habits.

Easily the worst habit is that of summarizing not the book's argument but its contents. Let us suppose you are reviewing a biography of Ernest Hemingway. The temptation is to write about Hemingway rather than about the book. This is a path to disaster. Hemingway had an eventful but widely known career. You are not, in all probability, going to find that much that is fresh or interesting to say about him. Meanwhile you have ignored your primary responsibility, which is to tell the reader what this study has to say that is fresh or interesting.

So you need to remind yourself as forcefully as possible that your job is to review the book and not the subject of the book. Does the book fix narrowly on Hemingway or does it also go into the literary circle to which he belonged? Is the author sympathetic to him? Does the writer attempt to psychoanalyze him or stick to questions of his style and themes? Is the book in firm command of the available evidence (this requires you to read the footnotes)? Does the author have something new to say about Hemingway and his times? If so, how well documented is this new interpretation?

You should generally not comment on whether you enjoyed the book. That is undoubtedly an important consideration for you, but it is of little interest to anyone else. There are occasions when you need to suffer in silence. This is one of them.

## HOW TO SELECT A
## TERM PAPER TOPIC

Doing research, as you may already have had occasion to learn, is hard work. It is sometimes boring.

Typically it involves long periods of going through material that is not what you were looking for and is not particularly interesting. It also involves taking detailed and careful notes, many of which you will never use. These are the dues you must pay if you are ever to earn the excitement that comes when you finally find the missing piece of evidence and make sense of things.

Not everything about doing research is boring. Aside from the indescribable sensation of actually finding out what you wanted to know are occasional happy accidents when you stumble across something that while not relevant to your research nonetheless pricks your imagination. Many a scholar studying an old political campaign has read up on the pennant races or fashions or radio listings for that year. These are, as one scholar puts it, oases in the desert of evidence. But, as he quickly adds, no one crosses the desert just to get to the oasis. The truth of the matter is that you have to have a good reason for getting to the other side. This means a topic you are genuinely interested in.

The point cannot be overemphasized. If you have a question you really want to answer, you will find it much easier to endure the tedium of turning all those pages. You will have a motive for taking good notes and for keeping your facts straight. If you are not interested in your topic, you are going to be constantly tempted to take shortcuts. And even if you resist temptation, you will find it hard to think seriously about what you do find.

So the topic has to interest you. That, you may be thinking, is easy to say. But what if your interest in the subject is less than compelling? Are you then going to be stuck with some topic you could care little about? The answer is No. No, that is, unless it turns out that you have no curiosity about anything at all; and if that is the case, you are probably dead already. Anything that can be examined chronologically is fair game for the historian. Histories exist of sports and of sciences, of sexual practices and jokes about them, of work and of recreation. Suppose the course is in literature. Can you find no poem, no novel, no body of literary criticism that has anything you want to talk about? Is sociology, or politics, or anthropology a dry creek? Surely your imagination can find a topic on which you and your instructor will agree. This being true, if you wind up writing on some question you are not passionately concerned with answering, you alone are at fault.

Once you have such a topic you need to find ways of defining it so that you can write an intelligent essay. "The Automobile in American Life" could serve as the subject for a very long book. It is not going to work as a subject for a term paper. You could not possibly search out so vast a topic in the time you have to work with. And your paper, however long, is not going to be of book length, so you would be stuck with trying to compress an immense amount of information into a brief essay. You need to fix on some element of the general topic that you can intelligently treat in the space and time you have to work with.

Students usually look at this problem backwards. They complain about how long their papers have to be. They should complain about how short they have to be. Space is a luxury you normally cannot afford. If you have done a fair amount of research on an interesting topic, your problem is going to be one of finding a way of getting into your paper all you have to say. Writing consists of choices about what you want to say. And if you have done your work properly, the hard choices involve deciding what to leave out.

"Fair enough," you may be thinking, "but I do not want to get stuck investigating some minute bit of trivia, the 'gear shift level from 1940 to 1953,' for example. I want to study the automobile in American life." Here we come to the core of the matter. Your topic must be narrowly defined so that you can do it justice, but it must also speak to the broad question that interested you in the first place. The trick is to decide just what it is about your topic—cars in this instance—that really interests you. Cars are means of transportation, of course, but they are also status symbols, examples of technology, and much else. Because of the automobile, cities and suburbs are designed in ways very different from how they were when people traveled by trolley or train. The automobile has dictated even teenage dating patterns. Having a driver's license, and regular access to a car, has become for some teenagers an obsession.

The point is that you have to think about your topic and then decide what within it to examine. If you end up doing a treatise on differing methods of changing tires, you are your own enemy. You could have been studying sex and sexism in automobile advertising.

## HOW TO LOCATE MATERIAL

Once you have worked up an interesting and practical topic for your term paper, you are ready to begin your research. For many students this means ambling over to the library and poking around in the computer catalog. This may not be the best way to begin. The librarians who catalog the library's holdings, while skilled professionals, cannot possibly anticipate the needs of every individual student. So they catalog books by their main subject headings and then include obvious cross-references. But much of what you need may not be obvious. So, for example, if you are interested in the causes of the Civil War, you will have no trouble finding under "U.S. History, Civil War" a title such as Kenneth Stampp's *And the War Came*. But will you find Roy Nichol's *Disruption of the American Democracy*? Your subject, however, may have a general guide, such as the *Harvard Guide to American History*. In that case, draw titles from it.

Now you have the beginnings of a decent bibliography. Your next act should be to introduce yourself to the research librarian. This person's specialty is helping people look for information. Yet many students never consult with a librarian. Do not pass up an opportunity to make your work easier. Often a librarian can point you to more specialized bibliographical guides, show you where to learn of the most recent books and articles, and help you refine your topic by indicating what questions are easiest to get information on.

You now have a reasonably extensive set of cards. And you can now safely consult the card catalog to see which of these titles your library has. Prepare yourself for some disappointments. Even good undergraduate libraries will not have everything you need. They will have some (unless your library is very weak or your topic esoteric). Almost all college libraries participate in the interlibrary loan system. This system, which the library staff will gladly explain to you, permits you to get virtually any title you could wish for. The only catch is that you must give the library enough lead time. For books and articles that are not especially rare this normally means from a day or two to two weeks.

## HOW TO TAKE NOTES

Sifting through the material you have found, you will need to take careful notes. As you do, you should write down on a notecard each piece of information you believe might prove relevant. For each piece of information you also will have to specify the full source.

Following these two bits of advice will save you much time and trouble. Finding information in your sources is trouble enough. You do not want to have to find it all over again when you sit down to write your paper. But this is often just what students have to do because they failed to write down some bit of data (which, perhaps, seemed only marginally important at the time) or took all of their notes on loose leaf paper and now must search through every page to find this one fact. It is far easier, over the long run, to have a separate card for each piece or group of closely related pieces of information. Tell yourself that you are the last of the big time spenders and can afford to use up index cards as though they were blank pieces of paper, which is what they are.

The general rule is that in compiling your research notes you should take extra care so that the actual writing will be as trouble-free as possible. It follows that you should take lots of notes. Do not try to determine in advance whether you are going to use a particular bit of data. Always give yourself the margin of safety. Similarly, do not try to decide in advance whether you will quote the source exactly or simply paraphrase it. If you take down the exact words, you can always decide to make the idea your own by qualifying it in various ways and putting it in your own words.

## WRITING TERM PAPERS AND OTHER ESSAYS

You have no doubt already learned that next to mastery of the subject matter nothing is more important for earning good grades than effective writing. You surely know people who despite weak study habits get high grades. The reason may be their ability to write well.

Students who are not among that relatively small group who write well sometimes think it unfair that writing skills should count so heavily. The course, some complain, is in biology, or geology, or European literature, and not expository writing, and so their prose should not influence their grade. But teachers continue to believe that the ability clearly and forcefully to express what you know is an indispensable measure of how well you have learned the subject. Writing well is an invaluable skill, and not only in college. Many of the most desirable jobs involve writing: correspondence, reports, memoranda. The writing will never stop.

No matter how poorly you write, if you can speak English effectively you can learn to write it effectively. It is simply a matter of expressing your ideas clearly. This you can learn to do. It requires not genius but merely patience and practice.

Charity, St. Paul said, is the chief of all the virtues. In expository prose, however, the chief virtue is clarity. And like charity, it covers a multitude of sins. If your sentences, however homely, are clear, they will receive a sympathetic reading.

It has perhaps crossed your mind that on some occasions you are not very eager to get to the point. Sometimes you may not be sure just what the point is. Sometimes you do know, but are not convinced that your point is a very good one. At such times, a little obfuscation may seem a better idea than clarity. It is not. Nothing is more troubling than reading a paper in which the author tried to hedge bets or fudge ideas. The very worst thing you can do is leave it up to your reader to decide what you are trying to say. So no matter how weak your ideas seem to you, set them forth clearly. Something is always better than nothing. Most teachers are interested in helping students. It is much easier to help you if your instructor can figure out what you were trying to say.

And teachers delight in watching students improve. The reason is obvious: They see it as proof that they are doing a good job. They take special pleasure in the progress of students who start off poorly but steadily get better over the course of the semester. You can do a lot worse than be one of those students.

I urge you, then, to give close attention to the advice this manual has offered on good writing. If you have the energy, learn to write gracefully. But in any event, write clearly.

## WHEN AND HOW TO USE FOOTNOTES

Many students apparently believe that the only thing worse than having to read footnotes is having to write them. It is easy to understand why they feel that way, but they are making much ado about very little. Footnotes inform the reader where the information in the body of the paper can be found. That is the substance of the matter.

So when should you use a footnote? One occasion is when you are referring to someone's exact words whether by direct quotation or by paraphrase. (If your paper does not require footnotes, you need only mention the author's name at the time you quote.) The other is when you are referring to some bit of information that is not already well known or is someone's interpretation of the facts. How, you might wonder, can you tell whether or not something is already well known? A simple rule is that nothing you can find in a standard textbook needs to be footnoted. Hence, for example, you do not have to footnote that George Washington was the first President of the United States. You may need to footnote an exact quotation from his "Farewell Address." You do not need to footnote that F. Scott Fitzgerald was the author of *The Great Gatsby*. If you are in doubt about a particular case, you still have two steps open to you. One is to ask your instructor, the reader you are seeking to inform in the first place. The other, if you find it impracticable to reach your teacher, is to use the footnote. Having an unnecessary footnote is a minor flaw. Not having a necessary one is a serious omission. So you can simply err on the safe side.

Now that you know when to use footnotes, you can consider the matter of how to use them. Several formats are in common use. Simply ask your instructor which one is preferred. If your teacher has no preference, invest in the inexpensive Modern Language Association (MLA) style sheet. It is brief, clearly written, reliable, and cheap. It is very unlikely you will encounter a question it will not answer.

## WHAT TO INCLUDE IN YOUR BIBLIOGRAPHY

Early in your research you compiled a list of possible sources. The temptation is to type out a bibliography from those cards. This is fine provided that you actually used all of those sources. Your bibliography should include all the sources you consulted and only those sources. So even though you have all sorts of cards, and even though your bibliography would look far more authoritative if you included sources you looked up but did not use, do not do so. It is most unlikely that padding your bibliography will impress.

## A WORD ABOUT PLAGIARISM AND ORIGINALITY

Plagiarism is the act of claiming another's work as your own. It is about as serious an academic offense as you can commit. Many colleges require teachers to report all instances of plagiarism, and while the punishment can vary, it is always stiff. And of all the various ways of cheating, teachers find plagiarism the easiest to detect.

Some students plagiarize without realizing that this is what they are doing. They quote from a book or article without so indicating by quotation marks or citing the author and the work, or they paraphrase a passage without proper acknowledgment. They have unintentionally passed off someone else's work as their own. Sometimes this results in nothing worse than a private lecture from the instructor on the necessity of correctly attributing all information. Even so it is embarrassing, and it creates the impression that you do not know what you are doing. So be sure you indicate the sources not only of your information but also of the interpretations or ideas you include in your papers.

Teachers will often tell their students that their papers should be original. Scholars use this word in a somewhat different sense from what you might expect. In ordinary speech something is original if it is the first of its kind or the only one of its kind. Scholars mean something less dramatic. We refer to research as "original" if the researcher did the work. We do not mean that the conclusions have never been reached before or that no one else has ever used the same source materials. The way you put together familiar information and ideas may be original.

Do not hesitate to make use of ideas from other scholars. No one with any sense expects beginning students to make startling discoveries or to develop radically new perspectives. It is, accordingly, perfectly legitimate for you to use other people's insights. The only hitch is that you must always acknowledge where they came from.

ADDITIONAL PAGES FOR ESSAY

ADDITIONAL PAGES FOR ESSAY

ADDITIONAL PAGES FOR ESSAY